W9-CQP-067

Poems:
Selected and New
1950–1974

By Adrienne Rich

ADRIENNE RICH

Poems
Selected and New
1950-1974

W · W · NORTON & COMPANY · INC ·
NEW YORK

"Moving in Winter" appeared originally in *American Poetry Now* (Critical Quarterly Supplement, n.d.) edited by Sylvia Plath; "The Parting: II" in *The Nation;* "Essential Resources" in *Sojourner;* "Blood-Sister" in *13th Moon;* "Re-Forming the Crystal" in *Field;* "Family Romance" in *Women/Poems* III; "From an Old House in America" in *Amazon Quarterly.*

Copyright © 1975, 1973, 1971, 1969, 1966 by
W. W. Norton & Company, Inc.

Copyright © 1967, 1963, 1962, 1961, 1960, 1959,
1958, 1957, 1956, 1955, 1954, 1953, 1952, 1951
by Adrienne Rich

Library of Congress Cataloging in Publication Data
Rich, Adrienne.
    Poems: selected and new, 1950–1974.
    I.   Title.
PS3535.I233A17   1974   811'.5'4   74–10781
ISBN 0–393–04392–4
ISBN 0–393–04395–9 (pbk.)

ALL RIGHTS RESERVED
Published simultaneously in Canada
by George J. McLeod Limited, Toronto

This book was designed by Robert Freese.
Typefaces used are Times Roman and Bodoni,
set by Spartan Typographers.
Printing was done by Murray Printing
and binding was done by The Haddon Craftsmen.
PRINTED IN THE UNITED STATES OF AMERICA

7 8 9 0

For Helen, my mother
and
for Cynthia, my sister

Contents

Contents   xiii

Foreword

I think of this book, not as a summing-up or even a retrospective, but as the graph of a process still going on. From the poems of seven volumes and nearly twenty-five years, I have chosen the ones that seem to me to belong, obliquely or not, most truly to that process. I've left out poems that felt more like exercises than poems, or that were written out of technique and habit rather than out of strangeness and necessity.

Also included are ten new poems, and eight written between 1957 and 1969, most unpublished until now.

In preparing the manuscript, I have made few alterations in old poems; those few have mainly to do with music and punctuation. Very rarely, I've altered a verb or a pronoun because I felt it had served as an evasion in the original version. (Such changes are detailed in the notes to the poems.) But I have not tried to remake the woman of twenty, or thirty, in the light of the woman of forty-five, or to revise my earlier experience and craft because I would see, and articulate, differently today.

I began dating poems sometime in 1954. I had come to the end of the kind of poetry I was writing in *The Diamond Cutters* and felt embarked on a process that was tentative and exploratory, both as to form and materials; I needed to allow the poems to speak for their moment. In arranging this manuscript I have been of course unable to date the earlier poems; they are therefore only roughly in chronological order.

As I type these words we are confronted with the naked and unabashed failure of patriarchal politics and patriarchal civilization. To be a woman at this time is to know extraordinary forms of anger, joy, impatience, love, and hope. Poetry, words on paper, are necessary but not enough; we need to touch the living who share our animal passion for existence, our determination that the sexual myths underlying the human condition can and shall be recognized and changed. My friends —above all, my sisters, the women I love—have given me the heat and friction of their lives, along with needed clarity, criticism, tenderness, and the daring of their examples. Midway in my own life, I know that we have only begun.

I have had an unusual male editor. I want to thank John Benedict: caring, painstaking, supportive in practical and intangible ways.

New York City, 1974

Adrienne Rich

From

A Change of World

1951

Storm Warnings

The glass has been falling all the afternoon,
And knowing better than the instrument
What winds are walking overhead, what zone
Of gray unrest is moving across the land,
I leave the book upon a pillowed chair
And walk from window to closed window, watching
Boughs strain against the sky

And think again, as often when the air
Moves inward toward a silent core of waiting,
How with a single purpose time has traveled
By secret currents of the undiscerned
Into this polar realm. Weather abroad
And weather in the heart alike come on
Regardless of prediction.

Between foreseeing and averting change
Lies all the mastery of elements
Which clocks and weatherglasses cannot alter.
Time in the hand is not control of time,
Nor shattered fragments of an instrument
A proof against the wind; the wind will rise,
We can only close the shutters.

I draw the curtains as the sky goes black
And set a match to candles sheathed in glass
Against the keyhole draught, the insistent whine
Of weather through the unsealed aperture.
This is our sole defense against the season;
These are the things that we have learned to do
Who live in troubled regions.

Aunt Jennifer's Tigers

Aunt Jennifer's tigers prance across a screen,
Bright topaz denizens of a world of green.
They do not fear the men beneath the tree;
They pace in sleek chivalric certainty.

Aunt Jennifer's fingers fluttering through her wool
Find even the ivory needle hard to pull.
The massive weight of Uncle's wedding band
Sits heavily upon Aunt Jennifer's hand.

When Aunt is dead, her terrified hands will lie
Still ringed with ordeals she was mastered by.
The tigers in the panel that she made
Will go on prancing, proud and unafraid.

Why Else But to Forestall This Hour

Why else but to forestall this hour, I stayed
Out of the noonday sun, kept from the rain,
Swam only in familiar depths, and played
No hand where caution signaled to refrain?

For fourteen friends I walked behind the bier;
A score of cousins wilted in my sight.
I heard the steeples clang for each new year,
Then drew my shutters close against the night.

Bankruptcy fell on others like a dew;
Spendthrifts of life, they all succumbed and fled.

I did not chide them with the things I knew:
Smiling, I passed the almshouse of the dead.

I am the man who has outmisered death,
In pains and cunning laid my seasons by.
Now I must toil to win each hour and breath;
I am too full of years to reason why.

Afterward

Now that your hopes are shamed, you stand
At last believing and resigned,
And none of us who touch your hand
Know how to give you back in kind
The words you flung when hopes were proud:
Being born to happiness
Above the asking of the crowd,
You would not take a finger less.
We who know limits now give room
To one who grows to fit her doom.

Boundary

What has happened here will do
To bite the living world in two,
Half for me and half for you.
Here at last I fix a line
Severing the world's design
Too small to hold both yours and mine.
There's enormity in a hair
Enough to lead men not to share
Narrow confines of a sphere
But put an ocean or a fence
Between two opposite intents.
A hair would span the difference.

An Unsaid Word

She who has power to call her man
From that estranged intensity
Where his mind forages alone,
Yet keeps her peace and leaves him free,
And when his thoughts to her return
Stands where he left her, still his own,
Knows this the hardest thing to learn.

Mathilde in Normandy

From the archaic ships the green and red
Invaders woven in their colored hosts
Descend to conquer. Here is the threaded headland,
The warp and woof of a tideless beach, the flight,
Recounted by slow shuttles, of swift arrows,
And the outlandish attitudes of death
In the stitched soldiery. That this should prove
More than the personal episode, more than all
The little lives sketched on the teeming loom
Was then withheld from you; self-conscious history
That writes deliberate footnotes to its action
Was not of your young epoch. For a pastime
The patient handiwork of long-sleeved ladies
Was esteemed proper when their lords abandoned
The fields and apple trees of Normandy
For harsher hunting on the opposite coast.
Yours was a time when women sat at home
To the pleasing minor airs of lute and hautbois,
While the bright sun on the expensive threads
Glowed in the long windless afternoons.
Say what you will, anxiety there too

Played havoc with the skein, and the knots came
When fingers' occupation and mind's attention
Grew too divergent, at the keen remembrance
Of wooden ships putting out from a long beach,
And the grey ocean dimming to a void,
And the sick strained farewells, too sharp for speech.

At a Bach Concert

Coming by evening through the wintry city
We said that art is out of love with life.
Here we approach a love that is not pity.

This antique discipline, tenderly severe,
Renews belief in love yet masters feeling,
Asking of us a grace in what we bear.

Form is the ultimate gift that love can offer—
The vital union of necessity
With all that we desire, all that we suffer.

A too-compassionate art is half an art.
Only such proud restraining purity
Restores the else-betrayed, too-human heart.

The Rain of Blood

In that dark year an angry rain came down
Blood-red upon the hot stones of the town.
Beneath the pelting of that liquid drought
No garden stood, no shattered stalk could sprout,
As from a sunless sky all day it rained
And men came in from streets of terror stained
With that unnatural ichor. Under night

Impatient lovers did not quench the light,
But listening heard above each other's breath
That sound the dying heard in rooms of death.
Each loudly asked abroad, and none dared tell
What omen in that burning torrent fell.
And all night long we lay, while overhead
The drops rained down as if the heavens bled;
And every dawn we woke to hear the sound,
And all men knew that they could stanch the wound,
But each looked out and cursed the stricken town,
The guilty roofs on which the rain came down.

Stepping Backward

Good-by to you whom I shall see tomorrow,
Next year and when I'm fifty; still good-by.
This is the leave we never really take.
If you were dead or gone to live in China
The event might draw your stature in my mind.
I should be forced to look upon you whole
The way we look upon the things we lose.
We see each other daily and in segments;
Parting might make us meet anew, entire.

You asked me once, and I could give no answer,
How far dare we throw off the daily ruse,
Official treacheries of face and name,
Have out our true identity? I could hazard
An answer now, if you are asking still.
We are a small and lonely human race
Showing no sign of mastering solitude
Out on this stony planet that we farm.
The most that we can do for one another
Is let our blunders and our blind mischances
Argue a certain brusque abrupt compassion.
We might as well be truthful. I should say
They're luckiest who know they're not unique;

But only art or common interchange
Can teach that kindest truth. And even art
Can only hint at what disturbed a Melville
Or calmed a Mahler's frenzy; you and I
Still look from separate windows every morning
Upon the same white daylight in the square.

And when we come into each other's rooms
Once in awhile, encumbered and self-conscious,
We hover awkwardly about the threshold
And usually regret the visit later.
Perhaps the harshest fact is, only lovers—
And once in a while two with the grace of lovers—
Unlearn that clumsiness of rare intrusion
And let each other freely come and go.
Most of us shut too quickly into cupboards
The margin-scribbled books, the dried geranium,
The penny horoscope, letters never mailed.
The door may open, but the room is altered;
Not the same room we look from night and day.

It takes a late and slowly blooming wisdom
To learn that those we marked infallible
Are tragi-comic stumblers like ourselves.
The knowledge breeds reserve. We walk on tiptoe,
Demanding more than we know how to render.
Two-edged discovery hunts us finally down;
The human act will make us real again,
And then perhaps we come to know each other.

Let us return to imperfection's school.
No longer wandering after Plato's ghost,
Seeking the garden where all fruit is flawless,
We must at last renounce that ultimate blue
And take a walk in other kinds of weather.
The sourest apple makes its wry announcement
That imperfection has a certain tang.
Maybe we shouldn't turn our pockets out
To the last crumb or lingering bit of fluff,

But all we can confess of what we are
Has in it the defeat of isolation—
If not our own, then someone's, anyway.

So I come back to saying this good-by,
A sort of ceremony of my own,
This stepping backward for another glance.
Perhaps you'll say we need no ceremony,
Because we know each other, crack and flaw,
Like two irregular stones that fit together.
Yet still good-by, because we live by inches
And only sometimes see the full dimension.
Your stature's one I want to memorize—
Your whole level of being, to impose
On any other comers, man or woman.
I'd ask them that they carry what they are
With your particular bearing, as you wear
The flaws that make you both yourself and human.

The Springboard

Like divers, we ourselves must make the jump
That sets the taut board bounding underfoot
Clean as an axe blade driven in a stump;
But afterward what makes the body shoot
Into its pure and irresistible curve
Is of a force beyond all bodily powers.
So action takes velocity with a verve
Swifter, more sure than any will of ours.

Unsounded

Mariner unpracticed,
In this chartless zone
Every navigator

Fares unwarned, alone.
Each his own Magellan
In tropics of sensation:
Not a fire-scorched stone
From prior habitation,
Not an archaic hull
Splintered on the beach.
These are latitudes revealed
Separate to each.

For the Conjunction of Two Planets

We smile at astrological hopes
And leave the sky to expert men
Who do not reckon horoscopes
But painfully extend their ken
In mathematical debate
With slide and photographic plate.

And yet, protest it if we will,
Some corner of the mind retains
The medieval man, who still
Keeps watch upon those starry skeins
And drives us out of doors at night
To gaze at anagrams of light.

Whatever register or law
Is drawn in digits for these two,
Venus and Jupiter keep their awe,
Wardens of brilliance, as they do
Their dual circuit of the west—
The brightest planet and her guest.

Is any light so proudly thrust
From darkness on our lifted faces

A sign of something we can trust,
Or is it that in starry places
We see the things we long to see
In fiery iconography?

From

The Diamond Cutters

1955

Ideal Landscape

We had to take the world as it was given:
The nursemaid sitting passive in the park
Was rarely by a changeling prince accosted.
The mornings happened similar and stark
In rooms of selfhood where we woke and lay
Watching today unfold like yesterday.

Our friends were not unearthly beautiful,
Nor spoke with tongues of gold; our lovers blundered
Now and again when most we sought perfection,
Or hid in cupboards when the heavens thundered.
The human rose to haunt us everywhere,
Raw, flawed, and asking more than we could bear.

And always time was rushing like a tram
Through streets of a foreign city, streets we saw
Opening into great and sunny squares
We could not find again, no map could show—
Never those fountains tossed in that same light,
Those gilded trees, those statues green and white.

The Tourist and the Town

San Miniato al Monte

Those clarities detached us, gave us form,
Made us like architecture. Now no more
Bemused by local mist, our edges blurred,
We knew where we began and ended. There
We were the campanile and the dome
Alive and separate in that bell-struck air,
Climate whose light reformed our random line,
Edged our intent and sharpened our desire.

15

Could it be always so: a week of sunlight,
Walks with a guidebook picking out our way
Through verbs and ruins, yet finding after all
The promised vista, once!—The light has changed
Before we can make it ours. We have no choice:
We are only tourists under that blue sky,
Reading the posters on the station wall:
Come, take a walking-trip through happiness.

There is a mystery that floats between
The tourist and the town. Imagination
Estranges it from her. She need not suffer
Or die here. It is none of her affair,
Its calm heroic vistas make no claim.
Her bargains with disaster have been sealed
In another country. Here she goes untouched,
And this is alienation. Only sometimes,
In certain towns she opens certain letters
Forwarded on from bitter origins,
That send her walking, sick and haunted, through
Mysterious and ordinary streets
That are no more than streets to walk and walk—
And then the tourist and the town are one.

To work and suffer is to be at home.
All else is scenery: the Rathaus fountain,
The skaters in the sunset on the lake
At Salzburg, or, emerging after snow,
The singular clear stars of Castellane.
To work and suffer is to come to know
The angles of a room, light in a square,
As convalescents learn the face of one
Who has watched beside them. Yours now, every street,
The noonday swarm across the bridge, the bells
Bruising the air above the crowded roofs,
The avenue of chestnut-trees, the road

To the post-office. Once upon a time
All these for you were fiction. Now, made free
You live among them. Your breath is on this air,
And you are theirs and of their mystery.

The Middle-aged

Their faces, safe as an interior
Of Holland tiles and Oriental carpet,
Where the fruit-bowl, always filled, stood in a light
Of placid afternoon—their voices' measure,
Their figures moving in the Sunday garden
To lay the tea outdoors or trim the borders,
Afflicted, haunted us. For to be young
Was always to live in other peoples' houses
Whose peace, if we sought it, had been made by others,
Was ours at second-hand and not for long.
The custom of the house, not ours, the sun
Fading the silver-blue Fortuny curtains,
The reminiscence of a Christmas party
Of fourteen years ago—all memory,
Signs of possession and of being possessed,
We tasted, tense with envy. They were so kind,
Would have given us anything; the bowl of fruit
Was filled for us, there was a room upstairs
We must call ours: but twenty years of living
They could not give. Nor did they ever speak
Of the coarse stain on that polished balustrade,
The crack in the study window, or the letters
Locked in a drawer and the key destroyed.
All to be understood by us, returning
Late, in our own time—how that peace was made,
Upon what terms, with how much left unsaid.

Lucifer in the Train

Riding the black express from heaven to hell
He bit his fingers, watched the countryside,
Vernal and crystalline, forever slide
Beyond his gaze: the long cascades that fell
Ribboned in sunshine from their sparkling height,
The fishers fastened to their pools of green
By silver lines; the birds in sudden flight—
All things the diabolic eye had seen
Since heaven's cockcrow. Imperceptibly
That landscape altered: now in paler air
Tree, hill and rock stood out resigned, severe,
Beside the strangled field, the stream run dry.

Lucifer, we are yours who stiff and mute
Ride out of worlds we shall not see again,
And watch from windows of a smoking train
The ashen prairies of the absolute.
Once out of heaven, to an angel's eye
Where is the bush or cloud without a flaw?
What bird but feeds upon mortality,
Flies to its young with carrion in its claw?
O foundered angel, first and loneliest
To turn this bitter sand beneath your hoe,
Teach us, the newly-landed, what you know;
After our weary transit, find us rest.

Living in Sin

She had thought the studio would keep itself;
no dust upon the furniture of love.
Half heresy, to wish the taps less vocal,

the panes relieved of grime. A plate of pears,
a piano with a Persian shawl, a cat
stalking the picturesque amusing mouse
had risen at his urging.
Not that at five each separate stair would writhe
under the milkman's tramp; that morning light
so coldly would delineate the scraps
of last night's cheese and three sepulchral bottles;
that on the kitchen shelf among the saucers
a pair of beetle-eyes would fix her own—
envoy from some village in the moldings . . .
Meanwhile, he, with a yawn,
sounded a dozen notes upon the keyboard,
declared it out of tune, shrugged at the mirror,
rubbed at his beard, went out for cigarettes;
while she, jeered by the minor demons,
pulled back the sheets and made the bed and found
a towel to dust the table-top,
and let the coffee-pot boil over on the stove.
By evening she was back in love again,
though not so wholly but throughout the night
she woke sometimes to feel the daylight coming
like a relentless milkman up the stairs.

The Insusceptibles

Then the long sunlight lying on the sea
Fell, folded gold on gold; and slowly we
Took up our decks of cards, our parasols,
The picnic hamper and the sandblown shawls
And climbed the dunes in silence. There were two
Who lagged behind as lovers sometimes do,
And took a different road. For us the night
Was final, and by artificial light
We came indoors to sleep. No envy there
Of those who might be watching anywhere
The lustres of the summer dark, to trace

Some vagrant splinter blazing out of space.
No thought of them, save in a lower room
To leave a light for them when they should come.

Holiday

Summer was another country, where the birds
Woke us at dawn among the dripping leaves
And lent to all our fêtes their sweet approval.
The touch of air on flesh was lighter, keener,
The senses flourished like a laden tree
Whose every gesture finishes in a flower.
In those unwardened provinces we dined
From wicker baskets by a green canal,
Staining our lips with peach and nectarine,
Slapping at golden wasps. And when we kissed,
Tasting that sunlit juice, the landscape folded
Into our clasp, and not a breath recalled
The long walk back to winter, leagues away.

Villa Adriana

When the colossus of the will's dominion
Wavers and shrinks upon a dying eye,
Enormous shadows sit like birds of prey,
Waiting to fall where blistered marbles lie.

But in its open pools the place already
Lay ruined, before the old king left it free.
Shattered in waters of each marble basin
He might have seen it as today we see.

Dying in discontent, he must have known
How, once mere consciousness had turned its back,

The frescoes of his appetite would crumble,
The fountains of his longing yawn and crack.

And all his genius would become a riddle,
His perfect colonnades at last attain
The incompleteness of a natural thing;
His impulse turn to mystery again.

Who sleeps, and dreams, and wakes, and sleeps again
May dream again; so in the end we come
Back to the cherished and consuming scene
As if for once the stones will not be dumb.

We come like dreamers searching for an answer,
Passionately in need to reconstruct
The columned roofs under the blazing sky,
The courts so open, so forever locked.

And some of us, as dreamers, excavate
Under the blanching light of sleep's high noon,
The artifacts of thought, the site of love,
Whose Hadrian has given the slip, and gone.

The Celebration in the Plaza

The sentimentalist sends his mauve balloon
Meandering into air. The crowd applauds.
The mayor eats ices with a cardboard spoon.

See how that color charms the sunset air;
A touch of lavender is what was needed.—
Then, pop! no floating lavender anywhere.

Hurrah, the pyrotechnic engineer
Comes with his sparkling tricks, consults the sky,
Waits for the perfect instant to appear.

Bouquets of gold splash into bloom and pour
Their hissing pollen downward on the dusk.
Nothing like this was ever seen before.

The viceroy of fireworks goes his way,
Leaving us with a sky so dull and bare
The crowd thins out: what conjures them to stay?

The road is cold with dew, and by and by
We see the constellations overhead.
But is that all? some little children cry.

All we have left, their pedagogues reply.

Autumn Equinox

The leaves that shifted overhead all summer
Are marked for earth now, and I bring the baskets
Still dark with clingings of another season
Up from the cellar. All the house is still,
Now that I've left it. Lyman in his study
Peers on a page of Dryden by the window,
Eyes alone moving, like a mended
Piece of old clockwork. When the afternoon
Trails into half-light, he will never notice
Until I come indoors to light the lamps
And rouse him blinking from the brownish type,
The gilt and tarnished spine of volume five
Out of the glass-doored cabinet in the hall.
Why Satires, I have wondered? For I've seen
The title-page, and riffled through the volume,
When he was gone. I thought that growing old
Returned one to a vague Arcadian longing,
To Ovid, Spenser, something golden-aged,
Some incorruptible myth that tinged the years
With pastoral flavors. Lyman, too, as gentle
As an old shepherd, half-apologetic
When I come bustling to disturb his dreams—

What in that bitterness can speak to him
Or help him down these final sloping decades
With kindly arm? I've never been a scholar—
Reader, perhaps at times, but not a scholar,
Not in the way that Lyman used to be—
And yet I know there's acid on the page
He pores—that least acidulous of men.
While I, who spent my youth and middle-age
In stubbornness and railing, pass the time
Now, after fifty, raking in the sun
The leaves that sprinkle slowly on the grass,
And feel their gold like firelight at my back,
In slow preoccupation with September.

Sometimes I call across to Alice Hume
And meet her at the fence as women meet
To say the weather's seasonably fine,
Talk husbands, bargains, or philosophize.
She thinks perhaps how sharp of tongue and quick
I used to be, and how I've quieted down,
Without those airs because I'd married Lyman,
Professor at the college, while her husband
Was just another farmer. That was pride
As raw and silly as the girl I was—
Reading too much, sneering at other girls
Whose learning was of cookery and flirtation.
Father would have me clever, sometimes said
He'd let me train for medicine, like a son,
To come into his practice. So I studied
German and botany, and hated both.
What good for me to know the Latin name
For huckleberry, while the others climbed
To pick the fruit and kissed across the bushes?
I never was a scholar, but I had
A woman's love for men of intellect,
A woman's need for love of any kind.

So Lyman came to ask me of my father:
Stiff-collared, shy, not quite the man I'd dreamed—
(Byron and Matthew Arnold vaguely mingled

Without the disadvantages of either.)
And yet he seemed superb in his refusal
To read aloud from Bryant to the ladies
Assembled on the boarding-house piazza
Among the moth-wings of a summer evening.
His quick withdrawal won my heart. I smile
Sometimes to think what quirks of vanity
Propel us toward our choices in the end.

The wedding-picture in the bureau drawer
Has on the back in Lyman's measured writing:
"September twenty-second, nineteen-twelve."
I keep it in its folder, deckle-edged
And yellowing. I see myself again,
Correct and terrified on our wedding-day,
Wearing the lace my mother wore before me
And buttoned shoes that pinched. I feel again
The trembling of my hand in Lyman's fingers,
Awkwardly held in that ungainly pose
While aunts around us nodded like the Fates
That nemesis was accomplished. Lyman stood
So thin and ministerial in his black,
I thought he looked a stranger. In the picture
We are the semblance of a bride and groom
Static as figures on a mantelpiece,
As if that moment out of time existed
Then and forever in a dome of glass,
Where neither dust nor the exploring fly
Could speck its dry immutability.

Thus I became his partner in a life
Annual, academic; we observed
Events momentous as the ceremony
To dedicate the chapel carillon
(Memorial to Edward Stephens Hodge,
Class of nineteen-fourteen). There we heard
Those sounds converge upon the rural air
That soon became familiar as a hinge
Creaking and never silenced. In our meadow

The angular young took up their bats and shouted
Throughout the afternoon, while I was pouring
Tea for the dean's arthritic wife. For Lyman
The world was all the distance he pursued
From home to lecture-room, and home again,
Exchanging nods with colleagues, smiling vaguely
Upon a shirtsleeved trio, tanned and jostling,
Who grinned and gave him room upon the path.
I bit my fingers, changed the parlor curtains
To ones the like of which were never seen
Along our grave and academic street.
I brought them home from Springfield in a bundle
And hung them in defiance. I took a walk
Across the fields one heavy summer night
Until the college from a mile away
Looked sallow, insignificant in the moonlight.
It seemed the moon must shine on finer things
I had not seen, things that could show with pride
Beneath that silver globe. Along the walls
Of Lyman's study there were steel engravings
Framed in black oak: the crazy tower of Pisa,
The Pyramids, rooted in desert sand,
Cologne Cathedral with its dangerous spires
Piercing the atmosphere. I hated them
For priggishly enclosing in a room
The marvels of the world, as if declaring
Such was the right and fitting rôle of marvels.

Night, and I wept aloud; half in my sleep,
Half feeling Lyman's wonder as he leaned
Above to shake me. "Are you ill, unhappy?
Tell me what I can do."

                "I'm sick, I guess—
I thought that life was different than it is."

"Tell me what's wrong. Why can't you ever say?
I'm here, you know."

                Half shamed, I turned to see

The lines of grievous love upon his face,
The love that gropes and cannot understand.

"I must be crazy, Lyman—or a dream
Has made me babble things I never thought.
Go back to sleep—I won't be so again."

Young lovers talk of giving all the heart
Into each others' trust: their rhetoric
Won't stand for analyzing, I'm aware,
But have they thought of this: that each must know
Beyond a doubt what's given, what received?

Now we are old like Nature; patient, staid,
Unhurried from the year's wellworn routine,
We wake and take the day for what it is,
And sleep as calmly as the dead who know
They'll wake to their reward. We have become
As unselfconscious as a pair of trees,
Not questioning, but living. Even autumn
Can only carry through what spring began.
What else could happen now but loss of leaf
And rain upon the boughs? So I have thought,
And wondered faintly where the thought began,
And when the irritable gust of youth
Stopped turning every blade of grass to find
A new dissatisfaction. Meanwhile Lyman
Reads satire in the falling afternoon—
A change for him as well. We finish off
Not quite as we began. I hear the bells
Wandering through the air across the fields.
I've raked three bushel baskets full of leaves—
Enough for one September afternoon.

The Prospect

You promise me when certain things are done
We'll close these rooms above a city square,

And stealing out by half-light, will be gone
When next the telephone breaks the waiting air.
Before they send to find us, we shall be
Aboard a blunt-nosed steamer, at whose rail
We'll watch the loading of the last brown bale
And feel the channel roughening into sea.

And after many sunlit days we'll sight
The coast you tell me of. Along that shore
Rare shells lie tumbled, and the seas of light
Dip past the golden rocks to crash and pour
Upon the bowl-shaped beach. In that clear bay
We'll scoop for pebbles till our feet and hands
Are gilded by the wash of blending sands;
And though the boat lift anchor, we shall stay.

You will discover in the woods beyond
The creatures you have loved on Chinese silk:
The shell-gray fox, gazelles that at your sound
Will lift their eyes as calm as golden milk.
The leaves and grasses feathered into plumes
Will shadow-edge their pale calligraphy;
And in the evening you will come to me
To tell of honey thick in silver combs.

Yet in the drift of moments unendeared
By sameness, when the cracks of morning show
Only a replica of days we've marred
With still the same old penances to do,
In furnished rooms above a city square,
Eating the rind of fact, I sometimes dread
The promise of that honey-breeding air,
Those unapportioned clusters overhead.

The Insomniacs

The mystic finishes in time,
The actor finds himself in space;

And each, wherever he has been,
Must know his hand before his face,
Must crawl back into his own skin
As in the darkness after crime
The thief can hear his breath again,
Resume the knowledge of his limbs
And how the spasm goes and comes
Under the bones that cage his heart.

So: we are fairly met, grave friend—
The meeting of two wounds in man.
I, gesturing with practiced hand,
I, my my great brocaded gown,
And you, the fixed and patient one,
Enduring all the world can do.
I, with my shifting masks, the gold,
The awful scarlet, laughing blue,
Maker of many worlds; and you,
Worldless, the pure receptacle.

And yet your floating eyes reveal
What saint or mummer groans to feel:
That finite creatures finally know
The damp of stone beneath the knees,
The stiffness in the folded hands
A duller ache than only wounds,
The draught that never stirs the sleeve
Of glazed evangelists above,
But drives men out from sacred calm
Into the violent, wayward sun.

My voice commands the formal stage;
A jungle thrives beyond the wings—
All formless and benighted things
That rhetoric cannot assuage.
I speak a dream and turn to see
The sleepless night outstaring me.
My pillow sweats; I wake in space.
This is my hand before my face.

This is the headboard of my bed
Whose splinters stuff my nightmare mouth;

This is the unconquerable drouth
I carry in my burning head.
Not my words nor your visions mend
Such infamous knowledge. We are split,
Done into bits, undone, pale friend,
As ecstasy begets its end;
As we are spun of rawest thread—
The flaw is in us; we will break.
O dare you of this fracture make
Hosannas plain and tragical,

Or dare I let each cadence fall
Awkward as learning newly learned,
Simple as children's cradle songs,
As untranslatable and true,
We someday might conceive a way
To do the thing we long to do—
To do what men have always done—
To live in time, to act in space
Yet find a ritual to embrace
Raw towns of man, the pockmarked sun.

A Walk by the Charles

Finality broods upon the things that pass:
Persuaded by this air, the trump of doom
Might hang unsounded while the autumn gloom
Darkens the leaf and smokes the river's glass.
For nothing so susceptible to death
But on this forenoon seems to hold its breath:
The silent single oarsmen on the stream
Are always young, are rowers in a dream.
The lovers underneath the chestnut tree,

Though love is over, stand bemused to see
The season falling where no fall could be.

You oarsmen, when you row beyond the bend,
Will see the river winding to its end.
Lovers that hold the chestnut burr in hand
Will speak at last of death, will understand,
Foot-deep amid the ruinage of the year,
What smell it is that stings the gathering air.

From our evasions we are brought at last,
From all our hopes of faithfulness, to cast
One look of recognition at the sky,
The unimportant leaves that flutter by.
Why else upon this bank are we so still?
What lends us anchor but the mutable?

O lovers, let the bridge of your two hands
Be broken, like the mirrored bridge that bends
And shivers on the surface of the stream.
Young oarsmen, who in timeless gesture seem
Continuous, united with the tide,
Leave off your bending to the oar, and glide
Past innocence, beyond these aging bricks
To where the Charles flows in to join the Styx.

The Snow Queen

Child with a chip of mirror in his eye
Saw the world ugly, fled to plains of ice
Where beauty was the Snow Queen's promises.
Under my lids a splinter sharp as his
Has made me wish you lying dead
Whose image digs the needle deeper still.

In the deceptive province of my birth
I had seen yes turn no, the saints descend,
Their sacred faces twisted into smiles,
The stars gone lechering, the village spring
Gush mud and toads—all miracles
Befitting an incalculable age.

To love a human face was to discover
The cracks of paint and varnish on the brow;
Soon to distrust all impulses of flesh
That strews its sawdust on the chamber floor,
While at the window peer two crones
Who once were Juliet and Jessica.

No matter, since I kept a little while
One thing intact from that perversity—
Though landscapes bloomed in monstrous cubes and coils.
In you belonged simplicities of light
To mend distraction, teach the air
To shine, the stars to find their way again.

Yet here the Snow Queen's cold prodigious will
Commands me, and your face has lost its power,
Dissolving to its opposite like the rest.
Under my ribs a diamond splinter now
Sticks, and has taken root; I know
Only this frozen spear that drives me through.

The Diamond Cutters

However legendary,
The stone is still a stone,
Though it had once resisted
The weight of Africa,
The hammer-blows of time
That wear to bits of rubble
The mountain and the pebble—
But not this coldest one.

Now, you intelligence
So late dredged up from dark
Upon whose smoky walls
Bison took fumbling form
Or flint was edged on flint—
Now, careful arriviste,
Delineate at will
Incisions in the ice.

Be serious, because
The stone may have contempt
For too-familiar hands,
And because all you do
Loses or gains by this:
Respect the adversary,
Meet it with tools refined,
And thereby set your price.

Be hard of heart, because
The stone must leave your hand.
Although you liberate
Pure and expensive fires
Fit to enamor Shebas,
Keep your desire apart.
Love only what you do,
And not what you have done.

Be proud, when you have set
The final spoke of flame
In that prismatic wheel,
And nothing's left this day
Except to see the sun
Shine on the false and the true,
And know that Africa
Will yield you more to do.

Letter from the Land of Sinners

I write you this out of another province
That you may never see:
Country of rivers, its topography
Mutable in detail, yet always one,
Blasted in certain places, here by glaciers,
There by the work of man.

The fishers by the water have no boast
Save of their freedom; here
A man may cast a dozen kinds of lure
And think his days rewarded if he sight
Now and again the prize, unnetted, flicking
Its prism-gleams of light.

The old lord lived secluded in his park
Until the hall was burned
Years ago, by his tenants; both have learned
Better since then, and now our children run
To greet him. Quail and hunter have forgotten
The echo of the gun.

I said there are blasted places: we have kept
Their nakedness intact—
No marble to commemorate an act
Superhuman or merely rash; we know
Why they are there and why the seed that falls there
Is certain not to grow.

We keep these places as we keep the time
Scarred on our recollection
When some we loved broke from us in defection,
Or we ourselves harried to death too soon
What we could least forgo. Our memories
Recur like the old moon.

But we have made another kind of peace,
And walk where boughs are green,
Forgiven by the selves that we have been,
And learning to forgive. Our apples taste
Sweeter this year; our gates are falling down,
And need not be replaced.

The Perennial Answer

The way the world came swinging round my ears
I knew what Doctor meant the day he said,
"Take care, unless you want to join your dead;
It's time to end this battling with your years."
He knew I'd have the blackest word told straight,
Whether it was my child that couldn't live,
Or Joel's mind, thick-riddled like a sieve
With all that loving festered into hate.
Better to know the ways you are accursed,
And stand up fierce and glad to hear the worst.
The blood is charged, the back is stiffened so.

Well, on that day that was a day ago,
And yet so many hours and years ago
Numbered in seizures of a darkening brain,
I started up the attic stairs again—
The fifth time in the hour—not thinking then
That it was hot, but knowing the air sat stiller
Under the eaves than when the idiot killer
Hid in the Matthews barn among the hay
And all the neighbors through one August day
Waited outside with pitchforks in the sun.
Joel waited too, and when they heard the gun
Resound so flatly in the loft above
He was the one to give the door a shove
And climb the ladder. A man not made for love,
But built for violence; he would stand
Where lightning flashed and watch with eyes so wide

You thought the prongs of fire would strike inside;
Or sit with some decaying book in hand,
Reading of spirits and the evil-eyed,
And witches' sabbaths in a poisoned land.

So it was Joel that brought the fellow out,
Tarnished with hay and blood. I still can see
The eyes that Joel turned and fixed on me
When it was done—as if by rights his wife
Should go to him for having risked his life
And say—I hardly knew what thing he wanted.
I know it was a thing I never granted,
And what his mind became, from all that woe,
Those violent concerns he lived among,
Was on my head as well. I couldn't go,
I never went to him, I never clung
One moment on his breast. But I was young.

And I was cruel, a girl-bride seeing only
Her marriage as a room so strange and lonely
She looked outside for warmth. And in what fashion
Could I be vessel for that somber passion—
For Joel, decreed till death to have me all?
The tortured grandsire hanging in the hall
Depicted by a limner's crabbed hand
Seemed more a being that I could understand.
How could I help but look beyond that wall
And probe the lawful stones that built it strong
With questions sharper than a pitchfork's prong?
If Joel knew, he kept his silence long.

But Evans and I were hopeless from the start:
He, collared early by a rigorous creed,
Not man of men but man of God indeed,
Whose eye had seen damnation, and whose heart
Thrust all it knew of passion into one
Chamber of iron inscribed *Thy will be done*.
Yet sense will have revenge on one who tries
To down his senses with the brand of lies.

The road was empty from the village home,
Empty of all but us and that dark third,
The sudden Northern spring. There must be some
For whom the thrusting blood, so long deferred
In alder-stem and elm, is not the rise
Of flood in their own veins; some who can see
That green unholy dance without surprise.
I only say it has been this for me:
The time of thinnest ice, of casualty
More swift and deadly than the skater's danger.
The end of March could make me stand a stranger
On my own doorstep, and the daily shapes
Of teapot, ladle, or the china grapes
I kept in winter on the dresser shelf
Rebuked me, made me foreign to myself.

Evans beside me on that moonless road
Walked hard as if he thought behind us strode
Pursuers he had fled through weary ways.
He only said: "Where I was born and grew,
You felt the spring come on you like a daze
Slow out of February, and you knew
The thing you were contending with. But here—"

"Spring is a bolt of lightning on the year,"
I said, "it strikes before you feel it near."

"The change of seasons is another thing
God put on earth to try us, I believe.
As if the breaking-out of green could bring
Escape from frozen discipline, give us leave
To taste of things by will and law forbidden."

"Maybe it was the weather lost us Eden,"
I said, but faltering, and the words went by
Like flights of moths under that star-soaked sky.
And that was all. He brought me to the door;
The house was dark, but on the upper floor
A light burned in the hallway. "Joel's asleep,"

I told him, and put out my hand. His touch
Was cold as candles kept unlit in church,
And yet I felt his seeking fingers creep
About my wrist and seize it in their grip
Until they hurt me.
                         "Neither you nor I
Have lived in Eden, but they say we die
To gain that day at last. We have to live
Believing it—what else can we believe?"

"Why not believe in life?" I said, but heard
Only the sanctioned automatic word
"Eternal life—" perennial answer given
To those who ask on earth a taste of heaven. .

The penalty you pay for dying last
Is facing those transactions from the past
That would detain you when you try to go.
All night last night I lay and seemed to hear
The to-and-fro of callers down below,
Even the knocker rattling on the door.
I thought the dead had heard my time was near
To meet them, and had come to tell me so;
But not a footstep sounded on the stair.
If they are gone it means a few days more
Are left, or they would wait. Joel would wait
Down by the dark old clock that told me late
That night from Boston. "Evans walked me home;
We sat together in the train by chance."
But not a word; only his burning glance.
"Why do you stand like that? What if I come
An hour or so after the time I said?
The house all dark, I thought you'd gone to bed."
But still that gaze, not anger, indignation,
Nor anything so easy, but a look
As fixed as when he stared upon his book.
No matter if my tale was false or true,
I was a woodcut figure on the page,
On trial for a nameless sin. Then rage

Took him like fire where lightning dives. I knew
That he could kill me then, but what he did
Was wrench me up the stairs, onto the bed.

The night of Joel's death I slept alone
In this same room. A neighbor said she'd stay,
Thinking the dead man lying down below
Might keep the living from rest. She told me so:
"Those hours before the dawn can lie like stone
Upon the heart—I've lain awake—I know."
At last I had to take the only way,
And said, "The nights he was alive and walking
From room to room and hearing spirits talking,
What sleep I had was likelier to be broken."
Her face was shocked but I was glad I'd spoken.
"Well, if you feel so—" She would tell the tale
Next morning, but at last I was alone
In an existence finally my own.

And yet I knew that Evans would find reason
Why we were not our own, nor had our will
Unhindered; that disturbance of a season
So long removed was something he would kill
Yet, if he had not killed it. When I stood
Beside the churchyard fence and felt his glance
Reluctantly compelling mine, the blood
Soared to my face, the tombstones seemed to dance
Dizzily, till I turned. The eyes I met
Accused as they implored me to forget,
As if my shape had risen to destroy
Salvation's rampart with a hope of joy.
My lips betrayed their *Why?* but then his face
Turned from me, and I saw him leave the place.
Now Joel and Evans are neighbors, down beneath.

I wonder what we're bound to after death?
I wonder what's exacted of the dead,
How many debts of conscience still are good?
Not Evans or his Bible ever said

That spirit must complete what flesh and blood
Contracted in their term. What creditors
Will wait and knock for us at marble doors?

I'd like to know which stays when life is past:
The marriage kept in fear, the love deferred,
The footstep waited for and never heard,
The pressure of five fingers round the wrist
Stopping its beat with pain, the mouth unkissed,
The dream whose waking startles into sight
A figure mumbling by the bed at night,
The hopeless promise of eternal life—
Take now your Scripture, Evans, if you will,
And see how flimsily the pages spill
From spines reduced to dust. What have they said
Of us, to what will they pronounce me wife?
My debt is paid: the rest is on your head.

From

Snapshots of a Daughter-in-Law

1963

Rural Reflections

This is the grass your feet are planted on.
You paint it orange or you sing it green,
    But you have never found
A way to make the grass mean what you mean.

A cloud can be whatever you intend:
Ostrich or leaning tower or staring eye.
    But you have never found
A cloud sufficient to express the sky.

Get out there with your splendid expertise;
Raymond who cuts the meadow does no less.
    Inhuman nature says:
Inhuman patience is the true success.

Human impatience trips you as you run;
    Stand still and you must lie.
It is the grass that cuts the mower down;
It is the cloud that swallows up the sky.

1956

The Knight

A knight rides into the noon,
and his helmet points to the sun,
and a thousand splintered suns
are the gaiety of his mail.
The soles of his feet glitter
and his palms flash in reply,

and under his crackling banner
he rides like a ship in sail.

A knight rides into the noon,
and only his eye is living,
a lump of bitter jelly
set in a metal mask,
betraying rags and tatters
that cling to the flesh beneath
and wear his nerves to ribbons
under the radiant casque.

Who will unhorse this rider
and free him from between
the walls of iron, the emblems
crushing his chest with their weight?
Will they defeat him gently,
or leave him hurled on the green,
his rags and wounds still hidden
under the great breastplate?

1957

Euryclea's Tale

I have to weep when I see it, the grown boy fretting
for a father dawdling among the isles,
and the seascape hollowed out by that boy's edged gaze
to receive one speck, one only, for years and years withheld.

And that speck, that curious man, has kept from home
till home would seem the forbidden place, till blood
and the tears of an old woman must run down
to satisfy the genius of place. Even then, what
can they do together, father and son?

the driftwood stranger and the rooted boy
whose eyes will have nothing then to ask the sea.

But all the time and everythere
lies in ambush for the distracted eyeball
light: light on the ship racked up in port,
the chimney-stones, the scar whiter than smoke,
than her flanks, her hair, that true but aging bride.

1958

The Loser

*A man thinks of the woman he
once loved: first, after her wedding,
and then nearly a decade later.*

1.

I kissed you, bride and lost, and went
home from that bourgeois sacrament,
your cheek still tasting cold upon
my lips that gave you benison
with all the swagger that they knew—
as losers somehow learn to do.

Your wedding made my eyes ache; soon
the world would be worse off for one
more golden apple dropped to ground
without the least protesting sound,
and you would windfall lie, and we
forget your shimmer on the tree.

Beauty is always wasted: if
not Mignon's song sung to the deaf,

at all events to the unmoved.
A face like yours cannot be loved
long or seriously enough.
Almost, we seem to hold it off.

2.

Well, you are tougher than I thought.
Now when the wash with ice hangs taut
this morning of St. Valentine,
I see you strip the squeaking line,
your body weighed against the load,
and all my groans can do no good.

Because you still are beautiful,
Though squared and stiffened by the pull
of what nine windy years have done.
You have three daughters, lost a son.
I see all your intelligence
flung into that unwearied stance.

My envy is of no avail.
I turn my head and wish him well
who chafed your beauty into use
and lives forever in a house
lit by the friction of your mind.
You stagger in against the wind.

1958

September 21

Wear the weight of equinoctial evening,
light like melons bruised on all the porches.
Feel the houses tenderly appraise you,
hold you in the watchfulness of mothers.

Once the nighttime was a milky river
washing past the swimmers in the sunset,
rinsing over sleepers of the morning.
Soon the night will be an eyeless quarry

where the shrunken daylight and its rebels,
loosened, dive like stones in perfect silence,
names and voices drown without reflection.

Then the houses draw you. Then they have you.

1958

Snapshots of a Daughter-in-Law

1.

You, once a belle in Shreveport,
with henna-colored hair, skin like a peachbud,
still have your dresses copied from that time,
and play a Chopin prelude
called by Cortot: *"Delicious recollections
float like perfume through the memory."*

Your mind now, moldering like wedding-cake,
heavy with useless experience, rich
with suspicion, rumor, fantasy,
crumbling to pieces under the knife-edge
of mere fact. In the prime of your life.

Nervy, glowering, your daughter
wipes the teaspoons, grows another way.

2.

Banging the coffee-pot into the sink
she hears the angels chiding, and looks out

past the raked gardens to the sloppy sky.
Only a week since They said: *Have no patience.*

The next time it was: *Be insatiable.*
Then: *Save yourself; others you cannot save.*
Sometimes she's let the tapstream scald her arm,
a match burn to her thumbnail,

or held her hand above the kettle's snout
right in the woolly steam. They are probably angels,
since nothing hurts her anymore, except
each morning's grit blowing into her eyes.

3.

A thinking woman sleeps with monsters.
The beak that grips her, she becomes. And Nature,
that sprung-lidded, still commodious
steamer-trunk of *tempora* and *mores*
gets stuffed with it all: the mildewed orange-flowers,
the female pills, the terrible breasts
of Boadicea beneath flat foxes' heads and orchids.

Two handsome women, gripped in argument,
each proud, acute, subtle, I hear scream
across the cut glass and majolica
like Furies cornered from their prey:
The argument *ad feminam,* all the old knives
that have rusted in my back, I drive in yours,
ma semblable, ma soeur!

4.

Knowing themselves too well in one another:
their gifts no pure fruition, but a thorn,
the prick filed sharp against a hint of scorn . . .
Reading while waiting
for the iron to heat,
writing, *My Life had stood—a Loaded Gun—*
in that Amherst pantry while the jellies boil and scum,

or, more often,
iron-eyed and beaked and purposed as a bird,
dusting everything on the whatnot every day of life.

5.

Dulce ridens, dulce loquens,
she shaves her legs until they gleam
like petrified mammoth-tusk.

6.

When to her lute Corinna sings
neither words nor music are her own;
only the long hair dipping
over her cheek, only the song
of silk against her knees
and these
adjusted in reflections of an eye.

Poised, trembling and unsatisfied, before
an unlocked door, that cage of cages,
tell us, you bird, you tragical machine—
is this *fertilisante douleur?* Pinned down
by love, for you the only natural action,
are you edged more keen
to prise the secrets of the vault? has Nature shown
her household books to you, daughter-in-law,
that her sons never saw?

7.

"To have in this uncertain world some stay
which cannot be undermined, is
of the utmost consequence."
                                        Thus wrote
a woman, partly brave and partly good,
who fought with what she partly understood.
Few men about her would or could do more,
hence she was labeled harpy, shrew and whore.

8.

"You all die at fifteen," said Diderot,
and turn part legend, part convention.
Still, eyes inaccurately dream
behind closed windows blankening with steam.
Deliciously, all that we might have been,
all that we were—fire, tears,
wit, taste, martyred ambition—
stirs like the memory of refused adultery
the drained and flagging bosom of our middle years.

9.

*Not that it is done well, but
that it is done at all?* Yes, think
of the odds! or shrug them off forever.
This luxury of the precocious child,
Time's precious chronic invalid,—
would we, darlings, resign it if we could?
Our blight has been our sinecure:
mere talent was enough for us—
glitter in fragments and rough drafts.

Sigh no more, ladies.
                    Time is male
and in his cups drinks to the fair.
Bemused by gallantry, we hear
our mediocrities over-praised,
indolence read as abnegation,
slattern thought styled intuition,
every lapse forgiven, our crime
only to cast too bold a shadow
or smash the mold straight off.

For that, solitary confinement,
tear gas, attrition shelling.
Few applicants for that honor.

10.

Well,
she's long about her coming, who must be
more merciless to herself than history.
Her mind full to the wind, I see her plunge
breasted and glancing through the currents,
taking the light upon her
at least as beautiful as any boy
or helicopter,

poised, still coming,
her fine blades making the air wince

but her cargo
no promise then:
delivered
palpable
ours.

1958–1960

Antinoüs: The Diaries

1959

Autumn torture. The old signs
smeared on the pavement, sopping leaves
rubbed into the landscape as unguent on a bruise,
brought indoors, even, as they bring flowers, enormous,
with the colors of the body's secret parts.
All this. And then, evenings, needing to be out,
walking fast, fighting the fire
that must die, light that sets my teeth on edge with joy,
till on the black embankment
I'm a cart stopped in the ruts of time.

Then at some house the rumor of truth and beauty
saturates a room like lilac-water

in the steam of a bath, fires snap, heads are high,
gold hair at napes of necks, gold in glasses,
gold in the throat, poetry of furs and manners.
Why do I shiver then? Haven't I seen,
over and over, before the end of an evening,
the three opened coffins carried in and left in a corner?
Haven't I watched as somebody cracked his shin
on one of them, winced and hopped and limped
laughing to lay his hand on a beautiful arm
striated with hairs of gold, like an almond-shell?

The old, needless story. For if I'm here
it is by choice and when at last
I smell my own rising nausea, feel the air
tighten around my stomach like a surgical bandage,
I can't pretend surprise. What is it I so miscarry?
If what I spew on the tiles at last,
helpless, disgraced, alone,
is in part what I've swallowed from glasses, eyes,
motions of hands, opening and closing mouths,
isn't it also dead gobbets of myself,
abortive, murdered, or never willed?

1959

Passing On

The landlord's hammer in the yard
patches a porch where your shirts swing
brashly against May's creamy blue.
This year the forsythia ran wild,
every bush a pile of sulfur.
Now, ragged, they bend
under the late wind's onslaught, tousled
as my head beneath the clotheslines.

Soon we'll be off. I'll pack us into parcels,
stuff us in barrels, shroud us in newspapers,
pausing to marvel at old bargain sales:
Oh, all the chances we never seized!
Emptiness round the stoop of the house
minces, catwise, waiting for an in.

1959

Merely to Know

1.

Wedged in by earthworks
thrown up by snouters before me,
I kick and snuffle, breathing in
cobwebs of beetle-cuirass:
vainglory of polished green,
infallible pincer, resonant nerve,
a thickening on the air now,
confusion to my lungs, no more.
My predecessors blind me—
their zeal exhausted among roots and tunnels,
they gasped and looked up once or twice
into the beechtree's nightblack glitter.

2.

Let me take you by the hair
and drag you backward to the light,
there spongelike press my gaze
patiently upon your eyes,
hold like a photographic plate
against you my enormous question.
What if you cringe, what if you weep?
Suffer this and you need suffer

nothing more. I'll give you back
yourself at last to the last part.
I take nothing, only look.
Change nothing. Have no need to change.
Merely to know and let you go.

1959

3.

Spirit like water
molded by unseen stone
and sandbar, pleats and funnels
according to its own
submerged necessity—
to the indolent eye
pure willfulness, to the stray
pine-needle boiling
in that cascade-bent pool
a random fury: Law,
if that's what's wanted, lies
asking to be read
in the dried brook-bed.

1961

Juvenilia

Your Ibsen volumes, violet-spined,
each flaking its gold arabesque . . .
Again I sit, under duress, hands washed,
at your inkstained oaken desk,
by the goose-neck lamp in the tropic of your books,
stabbing the blotting-pad, doodling loop upon loop,
peering one-eyed in the dusty reflecting mirror

of your student microscope,
craning my neck to spell above me

A DOLL'S HOUSE   LITTLE EYOLF
     WHEN WE DEAD AWAKEN

Unspeakable fairy tales ebb like blood through my head
as I dip the pen and for aunts, for admiring friends,
for you above all to read,
copy my praised and sedulous lines.

Behind the two of us, thirsty spines
quiver in semi-shadow, huge leaves uncurl and thicken.

1960

Double Monologue

To live illusionless, in the abandoned mine-
     shaft of doubt, and still
mime illusions for others? A puzzle
     for the maker who has thought
once too often too coldly.

Since I was more than a child
     trying on a thousand faces
I have wanted one thing: to know
     simply as I know my name
at any given moment, where I stand.

How much expense of time and skill
     which might have set itself
to angelic fabrications! All merely
     to chart one needle in the haymow?
Find yourself and you find the world?

Solemn presumption! Mighty Object
   no one but itself has missed,
what's lost, if you stay lost? Someone
   ignorantly loves you—will that serve?
Shrug that off, and presto!—

the needle drowns in the haydust.
   Think of the whole haystack—
a composition so fortuitous
   it only looks monumental.
There's always a straw twitching somewhere.

Wait out the long chance, and
   your needle too could get nudged up
to the apex of that bristling calm.
   Rusted, possibly. You might not want
to swear it was the Object, after all.

Time wears us old utopians.
   I now no longer think
"truth" is the most beautiful of words.
   Today, when I see "truthful"
written somewhere, it flares

like a white orchid in wet woods,
   rare and grief-delighting, up from the page.
Sometimes, unwittingly even,
   we have been truthful.
In a random universe, what more

exact and starry consolation?
   Don't think I think
facts serve better than ignorant love.
   Both serve, and still
our need mocks our gear.

1960

A Woman Mourned by Daughters

Now, not a tear begun,
we sit here in your kitchen,
spent, you see, already.
You are swollen till you strain
this house and the whole sky.
You, whom we so often
succeeded in ignoring!
You are puffed up in death
like a corpse pulled from the sea;
we groan beneath your weight.
And yet you were a leaf,
a straw blown on the bed,
you had long since become
crisp as a dead insect.
What is it, if not you,
that settles on us now
like satin you pulled down
over our bridal heads?
What rises in our throats
like food you prodded in?
Nothing could be enough.
You breathe upon us now
through solid assertions
of yourself: teaspoons, goblets,
seas of carpet, a forest
of old plants to be watered,
an old man in an adjoining
room to be touched and fed.
And all this universe
dares us to lay a finger
anywhere, save exactly
as you would wish it done.

1960

The Afterwake

Nursing your nerves
to rest, I've roused my own; well,
now for a few bad hours!
Sleep sees you behind closed doors.
Alone, I slump in his front parlor.
You're safe inside. Good. But I'm
like a midwife who at dawn
has all in order: bloodstains
washed up, teapot on the stove,
and starts her five miles home
walking, the birthyell still
exploding in her head.

Yes, I'm with her now: here's
the streaked, livid road
edged with shut houses
breathing night out and in.
Legs tight with fatigue,
we move under morning's coal-blue star,
colossal as this load
of unexpired purpose, which drains
slowly, till scissors of cockcrow snip the air.

1961

A Marriage in the 'Sixties

As solid-seeming as antiquity,
you frown above
the *New York Sunday Times*

where Castro, like a walk-on out of *Carmen,*
mutters into a bearded henchman's ear.

They say the second's getting shorter—
I knew it in my bones—
and pieces of the universe are missing.
I feel the gears of this late afternoon
slip, cog by cog, even as I read.
"I'm old," we both complain,
half-laughing, oftener now.

Time serves you well. That face—
part Roman emperor, part Raimu—
nothing this side of Absence can undo.
Bliss, revulsion, your rare angers can
only carry through what's well begun.

When
I read your letters long ago
in that half-defunct
hotel in Magdalen Street
every word primed my nerves.
A geographical misery
composed of oceans, fogbound planes
and misdelivered cablegrams
lay round me, a Nova Zembla
only your live breath could unfreeze.
Today we stalk
in the raging desert of our thought
whose single drop of mercy is
each knows the other there.
Two strangers, thrust for life upon a rock,
may have at last the perfect hour of talk
that language aches for; still—
two minds, two messages.

Your brows knit into flourishes. Some piece
of mere time has you tangled there.
Some mote of history has flown into your eye.

Will nothing ever be the same,
even our quarrels take a different key,
our dreams exhume new metaphors?
The world breathes underneath our bed.
Don't look. We're at each other's mercy too.

Dear fellow-particle, electric dust
I'm blown with—ancestor
to what euphoric cluster—
see how particularity dissolves
in all that hints of chaos. Let one finger
hover toward you from There
and see this furious grain
suspend its dance to hang
beside you like your twin.

1961

Attention

The ice age is here.
I sit burning cigarettes,
burning my brain.
A micro-Tibet,
deadly, frivolous, complete,
blinds the four panes.
Veils of dumb air
unwind like bandages
from my lips
half-parted, steady as the mouths
of antique statues.

1961

Sisters

Can I easily say,
I know you of course now,
no longer the fellow-victim,
reader of my diaries, heir
to my outgrown dresses,
ear for my poems and invectives?
Do I know you better
than that blue-eyed stranger
self-absorbed as myself
raptly knitting or sleeping
through a thirdclass winter journey?
Face to face all night
her dreams and whimpers
tangled with mine,
sleeping but not asleep
behind the engine drilling
into dark Germany,
her eyes, mouth, head
reconstructed by dawn
as we nodded farewell.
Her I should recognize
years later, anywhere.

1961

Peeling Onions

Only to have a grief
equal to all these tears!

There's not a sob in my chest.
Dry-hearted as Peer Gynt

I pare away, no hero,
merely a cook.

Crying was labor, once
when I'd good cause.
Walking, I felt my eyes like wounds
raw in my head,
so postal-clerks, I thought, must stare.
A dog's look, a cat's, burnt to my brain—
yet all that stayed
stuffed in my lungs like smog.

These old tears in the chopping-bowl.

1961

Peace

Lashes of white light
binding another hailcloud—
the whole onset all over
bursting against our faces,
sputtering like dead holly
fired in a grate:
And the birds go mad
potted by grapeshot
while the sun shines
in one quarter of heaven
and the rainbow
breaks out its enormous flag—
oily, unnegotiable—
over the sack-draped backs
of the cattle in their kingdom.

1961

The Roofwalker

—for Denise Levertov

Over the half-finished houses
night comes. The builders
stand on the roof. It is
quiet after the hammers,
the pulleys hang slack.
Giants, the roofwalkers,
on a listing deck, the wave
of darkness about to break
on their heads. The sky
is a torn sail where figures
pass magnified, shadows
on a burning deck.

I feel like them up there:
exposed, larger than life,
and due to break my neck.

Was it worth while to lay—
with infinite exertion—
a roof I can't live under?
—All those blueprints,
closings of gaps,
measurings, calculations?
A life I didn't choose
chose me: even
my tools are the wrong ones
for what I have to do.
I'm naked, ignorant,
a naked man fleeing
across the roofs
who could with a shade of difference
be sitting in the lamplight

against the cream wallpaper
reading—not with indifference—
about a naked man
fleeing across the roofs.

1961

Ghost of a Chance

You see a man
trying to think.

You want to say
to everything:
Keep off! Give him room!
But you only watch,
terrified
the old consolations
will get him at last
like a fish
half-dead from flopping
and almost crawling
across the shingle,
almost breathing
the raw, agonizing
air
till a wave
pulls it back blind into the triumphant
sea.

1962

Novella

Two people in a room, speaking harshly.
One gets up, goes out to walk.
(That is the man.)
The other goes into the next room
and washes the dishes, cracking one.
(That is the woman.)
It gets dark outside.
The children quarrel in the attic.
She has no blood left in her heart.
The man comes back to a dark house.
The only light is in the attic.
He has forgotten his key.
He rings at his own door
and hears sobbing on the stairs.
The lights go on in the house.
The door closes behind him.
Outside, separate as minds,
the stars too come alight.

1962

Prospective Immigrants Please Note

Either you will
go through this door
or you will not go through.

If you go through
there is always the risk
of remembering your name.

Things look at you doubly
and you must look back
and let them happen.

If you do not go through
it is possible
to live worthily

to maintain your attitudes
to hold your position
to die bravely

but much will blind you,
much will evade you,
at what cost who knows?

The door itself
makes no promises.
It is only a door.

1962

From

Necessities of Life

1966

Necessities of Life

Piece by piece I seem
to re-enter the world: I first began

a small, fixed dot, still see
that old myself, a dark-blue thumbtack

pushed into the scene,
a hard little head protruding

from the pointillist's buzz and bloom.
After a time the dot

begins to ooze. Certain heats
melt it.
         Now I was hurriedly

blurring into ranges
of burnt red, burning green,

whole biographies swam up and
swallowed me like Jonah.

Jonah! I was Wittgenstein,
Mary Wollstonecraft, the soul

of Louis Jouvet, dead
in a blown-up photograph.

Till, wolfed almost to shreds,
I learned to make myself

unappetizing. Scaly as a dry bulb
thrown into a cellar

I used myself, let nothing use me.
Like being on a private dole,

sometimes more like kneading bricks in Egypt.
What life was there, was mine,

now and again to lay
one hand on a warm brick

and touch the sun's ghost
with economical joy,

now and again to name
over the bare necessities.

So much for those days. Soon
practice may make me middling-perfect, I'll

dare inhabit the world
trenchant in motion as an eel, solid

as a cabbage-head. I have invitations:
a curl of mist steams upward

from a field, visible as my breath,
houses along a road stand waiting

like old women knitting, breathless
to tell their tales.

1962

In the Woods

"Difficult ordinary happiness,"
no one nowadays believes in you.

I shift, full-length on the blanket,
to fix the sun precisely

behind the pine-tree's crest
so light spreads through the needles
alive as water just
where a snake has surfaced,

unreal as water in green crystal.
Bad news is always arriving.
"We're hiders, hiding from something bad,"
sings the little boy.

Writing these words in the woods,
I feel like a traitor to my friends,
even to my enemies.
The common lot's to die

a stranger's death and lie
rouged in the coffin, in a dress
chosen by the funeral director.
Perhaps that's why we never

see clocks on public buildings any more.
A fact no architect will mention.
We're hiders, hiding from something bad
most of the time.

Yet, and outrageously, something good
finds us, found me this morning
lying on a dusty blanket
among the burnt-out Indian pipes

and bursting-open lady's-slippers.
My soul, my helicopter, whirred
distantly, by habit, over
the old pond with the half-drowned boat

toward which it always veers
for consolation: ego's Arcady:

leaving the body stuck
like a leaf against a screen.—

Happiness! how many times
I've stranded on that word,
at the edge of that pond; seen
as if through tears, the dragon-fly—

only to find it all
going differently for once
this time: my soul wheeled back
and burst into my body.

Found! Ready or not.
If I move now, the sun
naked between the trees
will melt me as I lie.

1963

The Corpse-Plant

> *How can an obedient man, or a sick man,*
> *dare to write poems?*
> *—Walt Whitman*

A milk-glass bowl hanging by three chains
from the discolored ceiling
is beautiful tonight. On the floor, leaves, crayons,
innocent dust foregather.

Neither obedient nor sick, I turn my head,
feeling the weight of a thick gold ring
in either lobe. I see the corpse-plants
clustered in a hobnailed tumbler

at my elbow, white as death, I'd say,
if I'd ever seen death;
whiter than life
next to my summer-stained hand.

Is it in the sun that truth begins?
Lying under that battering light
the first few hours of summer
I felt scraped clean, washed down

to ignorance. The gold in my ears,
souvenir of a shrewd old city,
might have been wearing thin as wires
found in the bones of a woman's head

miraculously kept in its essentials
in some hot cradle-tomb of time.
I felt my body slipping through
the fingers of its mind.

Later, I slid on wet rocks,
threw my shoes across a brook,
waded on algae-furred stones
to join them. That day I found

the corpse-plants, growing like
shadows on a negative
in the chill of fern and lichen-rust.
That day for the first time

I gave them their deathly names—
or did they name themselves?—
not "Indian pipes" as once
we children knew them.

Tonight, I think of winter,
winters of mind, of flesh,
sickness of the rot-smell of leaves
turned silt-black, heavy as tarpaulin,

obedience of the elevator cage
lowering itself, crank by crank
into the mine-pit,
forced labor forcibly renewed—

but the horror is dimmed:
like the negative of one
intolerable photograph
it barely sorts itself out

under the radiance of the milk-glass shade.
Only death's insect whiteness
crooks its neck in a tumbler
where I placed its sign by choice.

1963

The Trees

The trees inside are moving out into the forest,
the forest that was empty all these days
where no bird could sit
no insect hide
no sun bury its feet in shadow
the forest that was empty all these nights
will be full of trees by morning.

All night the roots work
to disengage themselves from the cracks
in the veranda floor.
The leaves strain toward the glass
small twigs stiff with exertion
long-cramped boughs shuffling under the roof
like newly discharged patients
half-dazed, moving
to the clinic doors.

I sit inside, doors open to the veranda
writing long letters
in which I scarcely mention the departure
of the forest from the house.
The night is fresh, the whole moon shines
in a sky still open
the smell of leaves and lichen
still reaches like a voice into the rooms.
My head is full of whispers
which tomorrow will be silent.

Listen. The glass is breaking.
The trees are stumbling forward
into the night. Winds rush to meet them.
The moon is broken like a mirror,
its pieces flash now in the crown
of the tallest oak.

1963

Like This Together

—for A.H.C.

1.

Wind rocks the car.
We sit parked by the river,
silence between our teeth.
Birds scatter across islands
of broken ice. Another time
I'd have said: "Canada geese,"
knowing you love them.
A year, ten years from now
I'll remember this—
this sitting like drugged birds

in a glass case—
not why, only that we
were here like this together.

2.

They're tearing down, tearing up
this city, block by block.
Rooms cut in half
hang like flayed carcasses,
their old roses in rags,
famous streets have forgotten
where they were going. Only
a fact could be so dreamlike.
They're tearing down the houses
we met and lived in,
soon our two bodies will be all
left standing from that era.

3.

We have, as they say,
certain things in common.
I mean: a view
from a bathroom window
over slate to stiff pigeons
huddled every morning; the way
water tastes from our tap,
which you marvel at, letting
it splash into the glass.
Because of you I notice
the taste of water,
a luxury I might
otherwise have missed.

4.

Our words misunderstand us.
Sometimes at night
you are my mother:

old detailed griefs
twitch at my dreams, and I
crawl against you, fighting
for shelter, making you
my cave. Sometimes
you're the wave of birth
that drowns me in my first
nightmare. I suck the air.
Miscarried knowledge twists us
like hot sheets thrown askew.

5.

Dead winter doesn't die,
it wears away, a piece of carrion
picked clean at last,
rained away or burnt dry.
Our desiring does this,
make no mistake, I'm speaking
of fact: through mere indifference
we could prevent it.
Only our fierce attention
gets hyacinths out of those
hard cerebral lumps,
unwraps the wet buds down
the whole length of a stem.

1963

Open-Air Museum

Ailanthus, goldenrod, scrapiron, what makes you flower?
What burns in the dump today?

Thick flames in a grey field, tended
by two men: one derelict ghost,

one clearly apter at nursing destruction,
two priests in a grey field, tending the flames
of stripped-off rockwool, split
mattresses, a caved-in chickenhouse,
mad Lou's last stack of paintings, each a perfect black lozenge

seen from a train, stopped
as by design, to bring us
face to face with the flag of our true country:
violet-yellow, black-violet,
its heart sucked by slow fire
O my America
this then was your desire?

but you cannot burn fast enough:
in the photograph the white
skirts of the Harlem bride
are lashed by blown scraps, tabloid sheets,
her beauty a scrap of flickering light
licked by a greater darkness

This then was your desire!
those trucked-off bad dreams
outside the city limits
crawl back in search of you, eyes
missing, skins missing, intenser in decay
the carriage that wheeled the defective baby
rolls up on three wheels
and the baby is still inside,
you cannot burn fast enough
Blue sparks of the chicory flower
flash from embers of the dump
inside the rose-rust carcass of a slaughtered Chevrolet
crouches the young ailanthus

and the two guardians go raking the sacred field, raking
slowly, to what endless end

Cry of truth among so many lies
at your heart burns on
a languid fire

1964

Two Songs

1.

Sex, as they harshly call it,
I fell into this morning
at ten o'clock, a drizzling hour
of traffic and wet newspapers.
I thought of him who yesterday
clearly didn't
turn me to a hot field
ready for plowing,
and longing for that young man
piercéd me to the roots
bathing every vein, etc.
All day he appears to me
touchingly desirable,
a prize one could wreck one's peace for.
I'd call it love if love
didn't take so many years
but lust too is a jewel
a sweet flower and what
pure happiness to know
all our high-toned questions
breed in a lively animal.

2.

That "old last act"!
And yet sometimes
all seems post coitum triste

and I a mere bystander.
Somebody else is going off,
getting shot to the moon.
Or, a moon-race!
Split seconds after
my opposite number lands
I make it—
we lie fainting together
at a crater-edge
heavy as mercury in our moonsuits
till he speaks—
in a different language
yet one I've picked up
through cultural exchanges . . .
we murmur the first moonwords:
Spasibo. Thanks. O.K.

1964

The Parting: I

The ocean twanging away there
and the islands like scattered laundry—

You can feel so free, so free,
standing on the headland

where the wild rose never stands still,
the petals blown off

before they fall
and the chicory nodding

blue, blue, in the all-day wind.
Barbed wire, dead at your feet,

is a kind of dune-vine,
the only one without movement.

Every knot is a knife
where two strands tangle to rust.

1963

Night-Pieces: For a Child

1. *The Crib*

You sleeping I bend to cover.
Your eyelids work. I see
your dream, cloudy as a negative,
swimming underneath.
You blurt a cry. Your eyes
spring open, still filmed in dream.
Wider, they fix me—
—death's head, sphinx, medusa?
You scream.
Tears lick my cheeks, my knees
droop at your fear.
Mother I no more am,
but woman, and nightmare.

2. *Her Waking*

Tonight I jerk astart in a dark
hourless as Hiroshima,
almost hearing you breathe
in a cot three doors away.

You still breathe, yes—
and my dream with its gift of knives,
its murderous hider and seeker,
ebbs away, recoils

back into the egg of dreams,
the vanishing point of mind.
All gone.

But you and I—
swaddled in a dumb dark
old as sickheartedness,
modern as pure annihilation—

we drift in ignorance.
If I could hear you now
mutter some gentle animal sound!
If milk flowed from my breast again. . . .

1964

After Dark

1.

You are falling asleep and I sit looking at you
old tree of life
old man whose death I wanted
I can't stir you up now.

Faintly a phonograph needle
whirs round in the last groove
eating my heart to dust.
That terrible record! how it played

down years, wherever I was
in foreign languages even
over and over, *I know you better*
than you know yourself   I know

you better than you know
yourself   I know

you   until, self-maimed,
I limped off, torn at the roots,

stopped singing a whole year,
got a new body, new breath,
got children, croaked for words,
forgot to listen

or read your *mene tekel* fading on the wall,
woke up one morning
and knew myself your daughter.
Blood is a sacred poison.

Now, unasked, you give ground.
We only want to stifle
what's stifling us already.
Alive now, root to crown, I'd give

—oh,—something—not to know
our struggles now are ended.
I seem to hold you, cupped
in my hands, and disappearing.

When your memory fails—
no more to scourge my inconsistencies—
the sashcords of the world fly loose.
A window crashes

suddenly down. I go to the woodbox
and take a stick of kindling
to prop the sash again.
I grow protective toward the world.

2.

Now let's away from prison—
Underground seizures!
I used to huddle in the grave
I'd dug for you and bite

my tongue for fear it would babble
—*Darling*—
I thought they'd find me there
someday, sitting upright, shrunken,

my hair like roots and in my lap
a mess of broken pottery—
wasted libation—
and you embalmed beside me.

No, let's away. Even now
there's a walk between doomed elms
(whose like we shall not see much longer)
and something—grass and water—

an old dream-photograph.
I'll sit with you there and tease you
for wisdom, if you like,
waiting till the blunt barge

bumps along the shore.
Poppies burn in the twilight
like smudge pots.
I think you hardly see me

but—this is the dream now—
your fears blow out,
off, over the water.
At the last, your hand feels steady.

1964

"I Am in Danger—Sir—"

"Half-cracked" to Higginson, living,
afterward famous in garbled versions,

your hoard of dazzling scraps a battlefield,
now your old snood

mothballed at Harvard
and you in your variorum monument
equivocal to the end—
who are you?

Gardening the day-lily,
wiping the wine-glass stems,
your thought pulsed on behind
a forehead battered paper-thin,

you, woman, masculine
in single-mindedness,
for whom the word was more
than a symptom—

a condition of being.
Till the air buzzing with spoiled language
sang in your ears
of Perjury

and in your half-cracked way you chose
silence for entertainment,
chose to have it out at last
on your own premises.

1964

Autumn Sequence

1.

An old shoe, an old pot, an old skin,
and dreams of the subtly tyrannical.
Thirst in the morning; waking into the blue

drought of another October
to read the familiar message nailed
to some burning bush or maple.

Breakfast under the pines, late yellow-
jackets fumbling for manna on the rim
of the stone crock of marmalade,

and shed pine-needles drifting
in the half-empty cup.
Generosity is drying out,

it's an act of will to remember
May's sticky-mouthed buds
on the provoked magnolias.

2.

Still, a sweetness hardly earned
by virtue or craft, belonging
by no desperate right to me

(as the marmalade to the wasp
who risked all in a last euphoria
of hunger)

washes the horizon. A quiet
after weeping, salt still on the tongue
is like this, when the autumn planet

looks me straight in the eye
and straight into the mind
plunges its impersonal spear:

Fill and flow over, think
till you weep, then sleep
to drink again.

3.

Your flag is dried-blood, turkey-comb
flayed stiff in the wind,
half-mast on the day of victory,

anarchist prince of evening marshes!
Your eye blurs in a wet smoke,
the stubble freezes under your heel,

the cornsilk *Mädchen* all hags now,
their gold teeth drawn,
the milkweeds gutted and rifled,

but not by you, foundering hero!
The future reconnoiters in dirty boots
along the cranberry-dark horizon.

Stars swim like grease-flecks
in that sky, night pulls a long knife.
Your empire drops to its knees in the dark.

4.

Skin of wet leaves on asphalt.
Charcoal slabs pitted with gold.
The reason for cities comes clear.

There must be a place, there has come a time—
where so many nerves are fusing—
for a purely moral loneliness.

Behind bloodsoaked lights of the avenues,
in the crystal grit of flying snow,
in this water-drop bulging at the taphead,

forced by dynamos three hundred miles
from the wild duck's landing and the otter's dive,
for three seconds of quivering identity.

There must be a place. But the eyeball stiffens
as night tightens and my hero passes out
with a film of stale gossip coating his tongue.

1964

Mourning Picture

The picture was painted by Edwin Romanzo Elmer
(1850–1923) as a memorial to his daughter Effie.
In the poem, it is the dead girl who speaks.

They have carried the mahogany chair and the cane rocker
out under the lilac bush,
and my father and mother darkly sit there, in black clothes.
Our clapboard house stands fast on its hill,
my doll lies in her wicker pram
gazing at western Massachusetts.
This was our world.
I could remake each shaft of grass
feeling its rasp on my fingers,
draw out the map of every lilac leaf
or the net of veins on my father's
grief-tranced hand.

Out of my head, half-bursting,
still filling, the dream condenses—
shadows, crystals, ceilings, meadows, globes of dew.
Under the dull green of the lilacs, out in the light
carving each spoke of the pram, the turned porch-pillars,
under high early-summer clouds,
I am Effie, visible and invisible,
remembering and remembered.

They will move from the house,
give the toys and pets away.

Mute and rigid with loss my mother
will ride the train to Baptist Corner,
the silk-spool will run bare.
I tell you, the thread that bound us lies
faint as a web in the dew.
Should I make you, world, again,
could I give back the leaf its skeleton, the air
its early-summer cloud, the house
its noonday presence, shadowless,
and leave *this* out? I am Effie, you were my dream.

1965

Halfway

—in memory: M.G.J.

In the field the air writhes, a heat-pocket.
Masses of birds revolve, blades
of a harvester.
The sky is getting milkily white,
a sac of light is ready to burst open.

Time of hailstones and rainbow.
My life flows North. At last I understand.
A young girl, thought sleeping, is certified dead.
A tray of expensive waxen fruit,
she lies arranged on the spare-room coverlid.

To sit by the fire is to become another woman,
red hair charring to grey,
green eyes grappling with the printed page,
voice flailing, flailing the uncomprehending.
My days lie open, listening, grandmother.

1965

The Knot

In the heart of the queen anne's lace, a knot of blood.
For years I never saw it,

years of metallic vision,
spears glancing off a bright eyeball,

suns off a Swiss lake.
A foaming meadow; the Milky Way;

and there, all along, the tiny dark-red spider
sitting in the whiteness of the bridal web,

waiting to plunge his crimson knifepoint
into the white apparencies.

Little wonder the eye, healing, sees
for a long time through a mist of blood.

1965

Moth Hour

Space mildews at our touch.
The leaves of the poplar, slowly moving—
aren't they moth-white, there in the moonbeams?
A million insects die every twilight,
no one even finds their corpses.
Death, slowly moving among the bleached clouds,
knows us better than we know ourselves.

I am gliding backward away from those who knew me
as the moon grows thinner and finally shuts its lantern.
I can be replaced a thousand times,
a box containing death.
When you put out your hand to touch me
you are already reaching toward an empty space.

1965

Focus

—*for Bert Dreyfus*

Obscurity has its tale to tell.
Like the figure on the studio-bed in the corner,

out of range, smoking, watching and waiting.
Sun pours through the skylight onto the worktable

making of a jar of pencils, a typewriter keyboard
more than they were. Veridical light . . .

Earth budges. Now an empty coffee-cup,
a whetstone, a handkerchief, take on

their sacramental clarity, fixed by the wand
of light as the thinker thinks to fix them in the mind.

O secret in the core of the whetstone, in the five
pencils splayed out like fingers of a hand!

The mind's passion is all for singling out.
Obscurity has another tale to tell.

1965

Face to Face

Never to be lonely like that—
the Early American figure on the beach
in black coat and knee-breeches
scanning the didactic storm in privacy,

never to hear the prairie wolves
in their lunar hilarity
circling one's little all, one's claim
to be Law and Prophets

for all that lawlessness,
never to whet the appetite
weeks early, for a face, a hand
longed-for and dreaded—

How people used to meet!
starved, intense, the old
Christmas gifts saved up till spring,
and the old plain words,

and each with his God-given secret,
spelled out through months of snow and silence,
burning under the bleached scalp; behind dry lips
a loaded gun.

1965

From

Leaflets

1969

Orion

Far back when I went zig-zagging
through tamarack pastures
you were my genius, you
my cast-iron Viking, my helmed
lion-heart king in prison.
Years later now you're young

my fierce half-brother, staring
down from that simplified west
your breast open, your belt dragged down
by an oldfashioned thing, a sword
the last bravado you won't give over
though it weighs you down as you stride

and the stars in it are dim
and maybe have stopped burning.
But you burn, and I know it;
as I throw back my head to take you in
an old transfusion happens again:
divine astronomy is nothing to it.

Indoors I bruise and blunder,
break faith, leave ill enough
alone, a dead child born in the dark.
Night cracks up over the chimney,
pieces of time, frozen geodes
come showering down in the grate.

A man reaches behind my eyes
and finds them empty
a woman's head turns away
from my head in the mirror
children are dying my death
and eating crumbs of my life.

Pity is not your forte.
Calmly you ache up there
pinned aloft in your crow's nest,
my speechless pirate!
You take it all for granted
and when I look you back

it's with a starlike eye
shooting its cold and egotistical spear
where it can do least damage.
Breathe deep! No hurt, no pardon
out here in the cold with you
you with your back to the wall.

1965

Holding Out

The hunters' shack will do,
abandoned, untended, unmended
in its cul-de-sac of alders.
Inside, who knows what
hovel-keeping essentials—
a grey saucepan, a broom, a clock
stopped at last autumn's last hour—
all or any, what matter.

The point is, it's a shelter,
a place more in- than outside.
From that we could begin.
And the wind is surely rising,
snow is in the alders.
Maybe the stovepipe is sound,
maybe the smoke will do us in
at first—no matter.

Late afternoons the ice
squeaks underfoot like mica,
and when the sun drops red and moon-
faced back of the gun-colored firs,
the best intentions are none too good.
Then we have to make a go of it
in the smoke with the dark outside
and our love in our boots at first—
no matter.

1965

In the Evening

Three hours chain-smoking words
and you move on. We stand in the porch,
two archaic figures: a woman and a man.

The old masters, the old sources,
haven't a clue what we're about,
shivering here in the half-dark 'sixties.

Our minds hover in a famous impasse
and cling together. Your hand
grips mine like a railing on an icy night.

The wall of the house is bleeding. Firethorn!
The moon, cracked every-which-way,
pushes steadily on.

1966

The Demon Lover

Fatigue, regrets. The lights
go out in the parking lot
two by two. Snow blindness
settles over the suburb.
Desire. Desire. The nebula
opens in space, unseen,
your heart utters its great beats
in solitude. A new
era is coming in.
Gauche as we are, it seems
we have to play our part.

A plaid dress, silk scarf,
and eyes that go on stinging.
Woman, stand off. The air
glistens like silk.
She's gone. In her place stands
a schoolgirl, morning light,
the half-grown bones
of innocence. Is she
your daughter or your muse,
this tree of blondness
grown up in a field of thorns?

Something piercing and marred.
Take note. Look back. When quick
the whole northeast went black
and prisoners howled and children
ran through the night with candles,
who stood off motionless
side by side while the moon swam up
over the drowned houses?
Who neither touched nor spoke?

whose nape, whose finger-ends
nervelessly lied the hours away?

A voice presses at me.
If I give in it won't
be like the girl the bull rode,
all Rubens flesh and happy moans.
But to be wrestled like a boy
with tongue, hips, knees, nerves, brain . . .
with language?
He doesn't know. He's watching
breasts under a striped blouse,
his bull's head down. The old
wine pours again through my veins.

Goodnight. then. 'Night. Again
we turn our backs and weary
weary we let down.
Things take us hard, no question.
How do you make it, all the way
from here to morning? I touch
you, made of such nerve
and flare and pride and swallowed tears.
Go home. Come to bed. The skies
look in at us, stern.
And this is an old story.

I dreamed about the war.
We were all sitting at table
in a kitchen in Chicago.
The radio had just screamed
that Illinois was the target.
No one felt like leaving,
we sat by the open window
and talked in the sunset.
I'll tell you that joke tomorrow,
you said with your saddest smile,
if I can remember.

The end is just a straw,
a feather furling slowly down,
floating to light by chance, a breath
on the long-loaded scales.
Posterity trembles like a leaf
and we go on making heirs and heirlooms.
The world, we have to make it,
my coexistent friend said, leaning
back in his cell.
Siberia vastly hulks
behind him, which he did not make.

Oh futile tenderness
of touch in a world like this!
how much longer, dear child,
do you think sex will matter?
There might have been a wedding
that never was:
two creatures sprung free
from castiron covenants.
Instead our hands and minds
erotically waver . . .
Lightness is unavailing.

Catalpas wave and spill
their dull strings across this murk of spring.
I ache, brilliantly.
Only where there is language is there world.
In the harp of my hair, compose me
a song. Death's in the air,
we all know that. Still, for an hour,
I'd like to be gay. How could a gay song go?
Why that's your secret, and it shall be mine.
We are our words, and black and bruised and blue.
Under our skins, we're laughing.

In triste veritas?
Take hold, sweet hands, come on . . .
Broken!

When you falter, all eludes.
This is a seasick way,
this almost/never touching, this
drawing-off, this to-and-fro.
Subtlety stalks in your eyes,
your tongue knows what it knows.
I want your secrets—I *will* have them out.
Seasick, I drop into the sea.

1966

Jerusalem

In my dream, children
are stoning other children
with blackened carob-pods
I dream my son is riding
on an old grey mare
to a half-dead war
on a dead-grey road
through the cactus and thistles
and dried brook-beds.

In my dream, children
are swaddled in smoke
and their uncut hair smolders
even here, here
where trees have no shade
and rocks have no shadow
trees have no memories
only the stones and
the hairs of the head.

I dream his hair is growing
and has never been shorn
from slender temples hanging

like curls of barbed wire
and his first beard is growing
smoldering like fire
his beard is smoke and fire
and I dream him riding
patiently to the war.

What I dream of the city
is how hard it is to leave
and how useless to walk
outside the blasted walls
picking up the shells
from a half-dead war
and I wake up in tears
and hear the sirens screaming
and the carob-tree is bare.

Balfour Street
July 1966

Charleston in the Eighteen-Sixties

Derived from the diaries of Mary Boykin Chesnut

He seized me by the waist and kissed my throat . . .
Your eyes, dear, are they grey or blue,
eyes of an angel?
The carts have passed already with their heaped
night-soil, we breathe again . . .
Is this what war is? Nitrate . . .
But smell the pear,
the jasmine, the violets.
Why does this landscape always sadden you?
Now the freshet is up on every side,
the river comes to our doors,
limbs of primeval trees dip in the swamp.

So we fool on into the black
cloud ahead of us.
Everything human glitters fever-bright—
the thrill of waking up
out of a stagnant life?
There seems a spell upon
your lovers,—all dead of wounds
or blown to pieces . . . Nitrate!
I'm writing, blind with tears of rage.
In vain. Years, death, depopulation, fears,
bondage—these shall all be borne.
No imagination to forestall woe.

1966

Night Watch

And now, outside, the walls
of black flint, eyeless.
How pale in sleep you lie.
Love: my love is just a breath
blown on the pane and dissolved.
Everything, even you,
cries silently for help, the web
of the spider is ripped with rain,
the geese fly on into the black cloud.
What can I do for you?
what can I do for you?
Can the touch of a finger mend
what a finger's touch has broken?
Blue-eyed now, yellow-haired,
I stand in my old nightmare
beside the track, while you,
and over and over and always you
plod into the deathcars.
Sometimes you smile at me

and I—I smile back at you.
How sweet the odor of the station-master's roses!
How pure, how poster-like the colors of this dream.

1967

For a Russian Poet

1. *The winter dream*

Everywhere, snow is falling. Your bandaged foot
drags across huge cobblestones, bells
hammer in distant squares.
Everything we stood against has conquered
and now we're part
of it all. *Life's the main thing,* I hear you say,
but a fog is spreading between this landmass
and the one your voice
mapped so long for me. All that's visible
is walls, endlessly yellow-grey, where
so many risks were taken, the shredded skies
slowly littering both our continents with
the only justice left, burying
footprints, bells and voices with all deliberate speed.

1967

2. *Summer in the country*

Now, again, every year for years: the life-and-death talk,
late August, forebodings
under the birches, along the water's edge
and between the typed lines

and evenings, tracing a pattern of absurd hopes
in broken nutshells
                    but this year we both

sit after dark with the radio
unable to read, unable to write

trying the blurred edges of broadcasts
for a little truth, taking a walk before bed
wondering what a man can do, asking that
at the verge of tears in a lightning-flash of loneliness.

3. *The demonstration*

"Natalya Gorbanevskaya
13/3 Novopeschanaya Street
Apartment 34

At noon we sit down quietly on the parapet
and unfurl our banners
                          almost immediately
the sound of police whistles
from all corners of Red Square
                                    we sit
quietly and offer no resistance—"

Is this your little boy—?

we will relive this over and over

the banners torn
from our hands
                  blood flowing
a great jagged torn place
in the silence of complicity

that much at least
we did here

In your flat, drinking tea
waiting for the police
your children asleep while you write
quickly, the letters you want to get off
before tomorrow

I'm a ghost at your table
touching poems in a script I can't read

we'll meet each other later

August 1968

Night in the Kitchen

The refrigerator falls silent.
Then other things are audible:
this dull, sheet-metal mind rattling like stage thunder.
The thickness budging forward in these veins
is surely something other
than blood:
say, molten lava.

You will become a black lace cliff fronting a deadpan sea;
nerves, friable as lightning
ending in burnt pine forests.
You are begun, beginning, your black heart drumming
slowly, triumphantly
inside its pacific cave.

1967

5:30 A.M.

Birds and periodic blood.
Old recapitulations.
The fox, panting, fire-eyed,
gone to earth in my chest.
How beautiful we are,

she and I, with our auburn
pelts, our trails of blood,
our miracle escapes,
our whiplash panic flogging us on
to new miracles!
They've supplied us with pills
for bleeding, pills for panic.
Wash them down the sink.
This is truth, then:
dull needle groping in the spinal fluid,
weak acid in the bottom of the cup,
foreboding, foreboding.
No one tells the truth about truth,
that it's what the fox
sees from her scuffled burrow:
dull-jawed, onrushing
killer, being that
inanely single-minded
will have our skins at last.

1967

Picnic

Sunday in Inwood Park
                    the picnic eaten
the chicken bones scattered
                         for the fox we'll never see
the children playing in the caves
My death is folded in my pocket
                         like a nylon raincoat
What kind of sunlight is it
                    that leaves the rocks so cold?

1967

The Book

—for Richard Howard

You, hiding there in your words
like a disgrace
the cast-off son of a family
whose face is written in theirs
who must not be mentioned
who calls collect three times a year
from obscure towns out-of-state
and whose calls are never accepted
You who had to leave alone
and forgot your shadow hanging under the stairs
let me tell you: I have been in the house
I have spoken to all of them
they will not pronounce your name
they only allude to you
rising and sitting, going or coming,
falling asleep and waking,
giving away in marriage or calling for water
on their deathbeds
their faces look into each other and see
you
when they write at night in their diaries they are writing
to you

1968

Abnegation

The red fox, the vixen
dancing in the half-light among the junipers,

wise-looking in a sexy way,
Egyptian-supple in her sharpness—
what does she want
with the dreams of dead vixens,
the apotheosis of Reynard,
the literature of fox-hunting?
Only in her nerves the past
sings, a thrill of self-preservation.
I go along down the road
to a house nailed together by Scottish
Covenanters, instinct mortified
in a virgin forest,
and she springs toward her den
every hair on her pelt alive
with tidings of the immaculate present.
They left me a westernness,
a birthright, a redstained, ravelled
afghan of sky.
She has no archives,
no heirlooms, no future
except death
and I could be more
her sister than theirs
who chopped their way across these hills
—a chosen people.

1968

Women

—*for C.R.G.*

My three sisters are sitting
on rocks of black obsidian.
For the first time, in this light, I can see who they are.

My first sister is sewing her costume for the procession.
She is going as the Transparent Lady
and all her nerves will be visible.

My second sister is also sewing,
at the seam over her heart which has never healed entirely.
At last, she hopes, this tightness in her chest will ease.

My third sister is gazing
at a dark-red crust spreading westward far out on the sea.
Her stockings are torn but she is beautiful.

1968

Implosions

*The world's
not wanton
only wild and wavering*

I wanted to choose words that even you
would have to be changed by

Take the word
of my pulse, loving and ordinary
Send out your signals, hoist
your dark scribbled flags
but take
my hand

All wars are useless to the dead

My hands are knotted in the rope
and I cannot sound the bell

My hands are frozen to the switch
and I cannot throw it

The foot is in the wheel

When it's finished and we're lying
in a stubble of blistered flowers
eyes gaping, mouths staring
dusted with crushed arterial blues

I'll have done nothing
even for you?

1968

On Edges

When the ice starts to shiver
all across the reflecting basin
or water-lily leaves
dissect a simple surface
the word *drowning* flows through me.
You built a glassy floor
that held me
as I leaned to fish for old
hooks and toothed tin cans,
stems lashing out like ties of
silk dressing-gowns
archangels of lake-light
gripped in mud.

Now you hand me a torn letter.
On my knees, in the ashes, I could never
fit these ripped-up flakes together.
In the taxi I am still piecing
what syllables I can
translating at top speed like a thinking machine
that types out *useless* as *monster*
and *history* as *lampshade*.

Crossing the bridge I need all my nerve
to trust to the man-made cables.

The blades on that machine
could cut you to ribbons
but its function is humane.
Is this all I can say of these
delicate hooks, scythe-curved intentions
you and I handle? I'd rather
taste blood, yours or mine, flowing
from a sudden slash, than cut all day
with blunt scissors on dotted lines
like the teacher told.

1968

The Observer

Completely protected on all sides
by volcanoes
a woman, darkhaired, in stained jeans
sleeps in central Africa.
In her dreams, her notebooks, still
private as maiden diaries,
the mountain gorillas move through their life term;
their gentleness survives
observation. Six bands of them
inhabit, with her, the wooded highland.
When I lay me down to sleep
unsheltered by any natural guardians
from the panicky life-cycle of my tribe
I wake in the old cellblock
observing the daily executions,
rehearsing the laws
I cannot subscribe to,
envying the pale gorilla-scented dawn

she wakes into, the stream where she washes her hair,
the camera-flash of her quiet
eye.

1968

Nightbreak

Something broken   Something
I need   By someone
I love   Next year
will I remember what
This anger   unreal
                              yet
has to be gone through
The sun to set
on this anger
                    I go on
head down   into it
The mountain pulsing
Into the oildrum   drops
the ball of fire.

Time is quiet   doesn't break things
or even wound   Things are in danger
from people   The frail clay lamps
of Mesopotamia
row on row under glass
in the ethnological section
little hollows for dried-
up oil   The refugees
with their identical
tales of escape   I don't
collect what I can't use   I need
what can be broken.

In the bed the pieces fly together
and the rifts fill   or else
my body is a list   of wounds
symmetrically placed
a village
blown open   by planes
that did not   finish the job
The enemy has   withdrawn
between raids   become invisible
there are
                no agencies
                        of relief
the darkness becomes utter
Sleep   cracked and flaking
sifts over the shaken   target

What breaks   is night
not day   The white
scar   splitting
over the east
The crack weeping
Time for the pieces
                        to move
dumbly back
                toward each other.

1968

Gabriel

There are no angels   yet
here comes an angel   one
with a man's face   young
shut-off   the dark
side of the moon   turning to me

and saying: *I am the plumed*
                serpent   the beast
                with fangs of fire   and a gentle
                heart

But he doesn't say that   His message
drenches his body
he'd want to kill me
for using words to name him

I sit in the bare apartment
reading
words stream past me   poetry
twentieth-century rivers
disturbed surfaces   reflecting clouds
reflecting wrinkled neon
but clogged   and mostly
nothing alive left
in their depths

The angel is barely
speaking   to me
Once in a horn of light
he stood   or someone like him
salutations in gold-leaf
ribboning from his lips
Today again   the hair streams
to his shoulders
the eyes reflect   something
like a lost country   or so I think
but the ribbon has reeled itself
up
    he *isn't giving*
or taking any shit
We glance miserably
across the room   at each other

It's true   there are moments
closer and closer together

when words stick   in my throat
                              the art of love
                              the art of words
I get your message Gabriel
just   will you stay looking
straight at me
awhile longer

1968

Leaflets

1.

The big star, and that other
lonely on black glass
overgrown with frozen
lesions, endless night
the Coal Sack gaping
black veins of ice on the pane
spelling a word:
                    Insomnia
not manic but ordinary
to start out of sleep
turning off and on
this seasick neon
vision, this
division

the head clears of sweet smoke
and poison gas

life without caution
the only worth living
love for a man
love for a woman

love for the facts
protectless

that self-defense be not
the arm's first motion

memory not only
cards of identity

that I can live half a year
as I have never lived up to this time—
Chekhov coughing up blood almost daily
the steamer edging in toward the penal colony
chained men dozing on deck
five forest fires lighting the island

lifelong that glare, waiting.

2.

Your face
            stretched like a mask
                                    begins to tear
as you speak of Che Guevara
Bolivia, Nanterre
I'm too young to be your mother
you're too young to be my brother

your tears are not political
they are real water, burning
as the tears of Telemachus
burned

Over Spanish Harlem the moon
swells up, a fire balloon
fire gnawing the edge
of this crushed-up newspaper

                                    now
the bodies come whirling

coal-black, ash-white
out of torn windows
and the death columns blacken
                whispering
Who'd choose this life?

We're fighting for a slash of recognition,
a piercing to the pierced heart.
Tell me what you are going through—

but the attention flickers and will flicker
a matchflame in poison air
a thread, a hair of light: sum of all answer
to the *Know that I exist!* of all existing things.

3.

If, says the Dahomeyan devil,
someone has courage to enter the fire
the young man will be restored to life.

If, the girl whispers,
I do not go into the fire
I will not be able to live with my soul.

(Her face calm and dark as amber
under the dyed butterfly turban
her back scarified in ostrich-skin patterns.)

4.

Crusaders' wind glinting
off linked scales of sea
ripping the ghostflags
galloping at the fortress
Acre, bloodcaked, lionhearted
raw vomit curdling in the sun
gray walkers walking
straying with a curbed intentness
in and out the inclosures

the gallows, the photographs
of dead Jewish terrorists, aged 15
their fading faces wide-eyed
and out in the crusading sunlight
gray strayers still straying
dusty paths
the mad who live in the dried-up moat
of the War Museum

what are we coming to
what wants these things of us
who wants them

5.

The strain of being born
      over and over has torn your smile into pieces
Often I have seen it broken
      and then re-membered
and wondered how a beauty
      so anarch, so ungelded
will be cared for in this world.
      I want to hand you this
leaflet streaming with rain or tears
      but the words coming clear
something you might find crushed into your hand
      after passing a barricade
and stuff in your raincoat pocket.
      I want this to reach you
who told me once that poetry is nothing sacred
      —no more sacred that is
than other things in your life—
      to answer yes, if life is uncorrupted
no better poetry is wanted.
      I want this to be yours
in the sense that if you find and read it
      it will be there in you already
and the leaflet then merely something
      to leave behind, a little leaf

in the drawer of a sublet room.
What else does it come down to
but handing on scraps of paper
little figurines or phials
no stronger than the dry clay they are baked in
yet more than dry clay or paper
because the imagination crouches in them.
If we needed fire to remind us
that all true images
were scooped out of the mud
where our bodies curse and flounder
then perhaps that fire is coming
to sponge away the scribes and time-servers
and much that you would have loved will be lost as well
before you could handle it and know it
just as we almost miss each other
in the ill cloud of mistrust, who might have touched
hands quickly, shared food or given blood
for each other. I am thinking how we can use what we have
to invent what we need.

Winter–Spring 1968

Ghazals: Homage to Ghalib

7/12/68

—for Sheila Rotner

The clouds are electric in this university.
The lovers astride the tractor burn fissures through the hay.

When I look at that wall I shall think of you
and of what you did not paint there.

Only the truth makes the pain of lifting a hand worthwhile:
the prism staggering under the blows of the raga.

The vanishing-point is the point where he appears.
Two parallel tracks converge, yet there has been no wreck.

To mutilate privacy with a single foolish syllable
is to throw away the search for the one necessary word.

When you read these lines, think of me
and of what I have not written here.

7/13/68

The ones who camped on the slopes, below the bare summit,
saw differently from us, who breathed thin air and kept walking.

Sleeping back-to-back, man and woman, we were more conscious
than either of us awake and alone in the world.

These words are vapor-trails of a plane that has vanished;
by the time I write them out, they are whispering something else.

Do we still have to feel jealous of our creations?
Once they might have outlived us; in this world, we'll die together.

Don't look for me in the room I've left;
the photograph shows just a white rocking-chair, still rocking.

7/14/68: i

In Central Park we talked of our own cowardice.
How many times a day, in this city, are those words spoken?

The tears of the universe aren't all stars, Danton;
some are satellites of brushed aluminum and stainless steel.

He, who was temporary, has joined eternity;
he has deserted us, gone over to the other side.

In the Theatre of the Dust no actor becomes famous.
In the last scene they all are blown away like dust.

"It may be if I had known them I would have loved them."
You were American, Whitman, and those words are yours.

7/14/68: ii

Did you think I was talking about my life?
I was trying to drive a tradition up against the wall.

The field they burned over is greener than all the rest.
You have to watch it, he said, the sparks can travel the roots.

Shot back into this earth's atmosphere
our children's children may photograph these stones.

In the red wash of the darkroom, I see myself clearly;
when the print is developed and handed about, the face
                                    is nothing to me.

For us the work undoes itself over and over:
the grass grows back, the dust collects, the scar breaks open.

7/16/68: i

Blacked-out on a wagon, part of my life cut out forever—
five green hours and forty violet minutes.

A cold spring slowed our lilacs, till a surf broke
violet/white, tender and sensual, misread it if you dare.

I tell you, truth is, at the moment, here
burning outward through our skins.

Eternity streams through my body:
touch it with your hand and see.

Till the walls of the tunnel cave in
and the black river walks on our faces.

7/16/68: ii

When they mow the fields, I see the world reformed
as if by snow, or fire, or physical desire.

First snow. Death of the city. Ghosts in the air.
Your shade among the shadows, interviewing the mist.

The mail came every day, but letters were missing;
by this I knew things were not what they ought to be.

The trees in the long park blurring back
into Olmsted's original dream-work.

The impartial scholar writes me from under house arrest.
I hope you are rotting in hell, Montaigne you bastard.

7/17/68

Armitage of scrap-iron for the radiations of a moon.
Flower cast in metal, Picasso-woman, sister.

Two hesitant Luna moths regard each other
with the spots on their wings: fascinated.

To resign *yourself*—what an act of betrayal!
—to throw a runaway spirit back to the dogs.

When the ebb-tide pulls hard enough, we are all starfish.
The moon has her way with us, my companion in crime.

At the Aquarium that day, between the white whale's loneliness
and the groupers' mass promiscuities, only ourselves.

7/23/68

When your sperm enters me, it is altered;
when my thought absorbs yours, a world begins.

If the mind of the teacher is not in love with the mind of the student,
he is simply practicing rape, and deserves at best our pity.

To live outside the law! Or, barely within it,
a twig on boiling waters, enclosed inside a bubble.

Our words are jammed in an electronic jungle;
sometimes, though, they rise and wheel croaking above the treetops.

An open window; thick summer night; electric fences trilling.
What are you doing here at the edge of the death-camps, Vivaldi?

7/24/68: i

The sapling springs, the milkweed blooms: obsolete Nature.
In the woods I have a vision of asphalt, blindly lingering.

I hardly know the names of the weeds I love.
I have forgotten the names of so many flowers.

I can't live at the hems of that tradition—
will I last to try the beginning of the next?

Killing is different now: no fingers round the throat.
No one feels the wetness of the blood on his hands.

When we fuck, there too are we remoter
than the fucking bodies of lovers used to be?

How many men have touched me with their eyes
more hotly than they later touched me with their lips.

7/24/68: ii

The friend I can trust is the one who will let me have my death.
The rest are actors who want me to stay and further the plot.

At the drive-in movie, above the PanaVision,
beyond the projector beams, you project yourself, great Star.

The eye that used to watch us is dead, but open.
Sometimes I still have a sense of being followed.

How long will we be waiting for the police?
How long must I wonder which of my friends would hide me?

Driving at night I feel the Milky Way
streaming above me like the graph of a cry.

7/26/68: i

Last night you wrote on the wall: Revolution is poetry.
Today you needn't write; the wall has tumbled down.

We were taught to respect the appearance behind the reality.
Our senses were out on parole, under surveillance.

A pair of eyes imprisoned for years inside my skull
is burning its way outward, the headaches are terrible.

I'm walking through a rubble of broken sculpture, stumbling
here on the spine of a friend, there on the hand of a brother.

All those joinings! and yet we fought so hard to be unique.
Neither alone, nor in anyone's arms, will we end up sleeping.

7/26/: ii

A dead mosquito, flattened against a door;
his image could survive our comings and our goings.

LeRoi! Eldridge! listen to us, we are ghosts
condemned to haunt the cities where you want to be at home.

The white children turn black on the negative.
The summer clouds blacken inside the camera-skull.

Every mistake that can be made, we are prepared to make;
anything less would fall short of the reality we're dreaming.

Someone has always been desperate, now it's our turn—
we who were free to weep for Othello and laugh at Caliban.

I have learned to smell a *conservateur* a mile away:
they carry illustrated catalogues of all that there is to lose.

7/26/68: iii

So many minds in search of bodies
groping their way among artificial limbs.

Of late they write me how they are getting on:
desertion, desertion, is the story of those pages.

A chewed-up nail, the past, splitting yet growing,
the same and not the same; a nervous habit never shaken.

Those stays of tooled whalebone in the Salem museum—
erotic scrimshaw, practical even in lust.

Whoever thought of inserting a ship in a bottle?
Long weeks without women do this to a man.

8/1/68

The order of the small town on the riverbank,
forever at war with the order of the dark and starlit soul.

Were you free then all along, Jim, free at last,
of everything but the white boy's fantasies?

We pleaded guilty till we saw what rectitude was like:
its washed hands, and dead nerve, and sclerotic eye.

I long ago stopped dreaming of pure justice, your honor—
my crime was to believe we could make cruelty obsolete.

The body has been exhumed from the burnt-out bunker;
the teeth counted, the contents of the stomach told over.

And you, Custer, the Squaw-killer, hero of primitive schoolrooms—
where are you buried, what is the condition of your bones?

8/4/68

—for Aijaz Ahmad

If these are letters, they will have to be misread.
If scribblings on a wall, they must tangle with all the others.

Fuck reds   Black Power   Angel loves Rosita
—and a transistor radio answers in Spanish: *Night must fall.*

Prisoners, soldiers, crouching as always, writing,
explaining the unforgivable to a wife, a mother, a lover.

Those faces are blurred and some have turned away
to which I used to address myself so hotly.

How is it, Ghalib, that your grief, resurrected in pieces,
has found its way to this room from your dark house in Delhi?

When they read this poem of mine, they are translators.
Every existence speaks a language of its own.

8/8/68: i

From here on, all of us will be living
like Galileo turning his first tube at the stars.

Obey the little laws and break the great ones
is the preamble to their constitution.

Even to hope is to leap into the unknown,
under the mocking eyes of the way things are.

There's a war on earth, and in the skull, and in the glassy spaces,
between the existing and the non-existing.

I need to live each day through, have them and know them all,
though I can see from here where I'll be standing at the end.

8/8/68: ii

—for A.H.C.

A piece of thread ripped-out from a fierce design,
some weaving figured as magic against oppression.

I'm speaking to you as a woman to a man:
when your blood flows I want to hold you in my arms.

How did we get caught up fighting this forest fire,
we, who were only looking for a still place in the woods?

How frail we are, and yet, dispersed, always returning,
the barnacles they keep scraping from the warship's hull.

The hairs on your breast curl so lightly as you lie there,
while the strong heart goes on pounding in its sleep.

Uncollected Poems

1957–1969

Moving in Winter

Their life, collapsed like unplayed cards,
is carried piecemeal through the snow:
Headboard and footboard now, the bed
where she has lain desiring him
where overhead his sleep will build
its canopy to smother her once more;
their table, by four elbows worn
evening after evening while the wax runs down;
mirrors grey with reflecting them,
bureaus coffining from the cold
things that can shuffle in a drawer,
carpets rolled up around those echoes
which, shaken out, take wing and breed
new altercations, the old silences.

1957

To Judith, Taking Leave

—for J.H.

Dull-headed, with dull fingers
I patch once more
the pale brown envelope
still showing under ink scratches
the letterhead of MIND.
A chorus of old postmarks
echoes across its face.
It looks so frail
to send so far

and I should tear it across
mindlessly
and find another.
But I'm tired, can't endure
a single new motion
or room or object,
so I cling to this too
as if your tallness moving
against the rainlight
in an Amsterdam flat
might be held awhile
by a handwritten label
or a battered envelope
from your desk.

Once somewhere else
I shan't talk of you
as a singular event
or a beautiful thing I saw
though both are true.
I shan't falsify you
through praising and describing
as I shall other
things I have loved
almost as much.
There in Amsterdam
you'll be living as I
have seen you live
and as I've never seen you.
And I can trust
no plane to bring you
my life out there
in turbid America—
my own life, lived against
facts I keep there.

It wasn't literacy—
the right to read MIND—
or suffrage—to vote

for the lesser of two
evils—that were
the great gains, I see now,
when I think of all those women
who suffered ridicule
for us.
But this little piece of ground,
Judith! that two women
in love to the nerves' limit
with two men—
shared out in pieces
to men, children, memories
so different and so draining—
should think it possible
now for the first time
perhaps, to love each other
neither as fellow-victims
nor as a temporary
shadow of something better.
Still shared-out as we are,
lovers, poets, warmers
of men and children
against our flesh, not knowing
from day to day
what we'll fling out on the water
or what pick up
there at the tide's lip,
often tired, as I'm tired now
from sheer distances of soul
we have in one day to cover—
still to get here
to this little spur or headland
and feel now free enough
to leave our weapons somewhere
else—such are the secret
outcomes of revolution!
that two women can meet
no longer as cramped sharers
of a bitter mutual secret

but as two eyes in one brow
receiving at one moment
the rainbow of the world.

1962

Roots

—for M.L.

Evenings seem endless, now
dark tugs at our sky
harder and earlier
and milkweeds swell to bursting . . .
now in my transatlantic eye
you stand on your terrace
a scarf on your head and in your hands
dead stalks of golden-glow

and now it's for you,
not myself, I shiver
hearing glass doors rattle
at your back, the rustling cough
of a dry clematis vine
your love and toil trained up the walls
of a rented house.

All those roots, Margo!
Didn't you start each slip between your breasts,
each dry seed, carrying some
across frontiers, knotted
into your handkerchief,
haven't you seen your tears
glisten in narrow trenches
where rooted cuttings grope for life?

You, frailer than you look,
long back, long stride, blond hair
coiled up over straight shoulders—
I hear in your ear the wind
lashing in wet from the North Sea
slamming the dahlias flat.
All your work violated
every autumn, every turn of the wrist
guiding the trowel: mocked.
Sleet on brown fibers,
black wilt eating your harvest,
a clean sweep, and you the loser . . .

or is this after all
the liberation your hands fend off
and your eyes implore
when you dream of sudden death
or of beginning anew,
a girl of seventeen, the war just over,
and all the gardens
to dig again?

1963

The Parting: II

White morning flows into the mirror.
Her eye, still old with sleep,
meets itself like a sister.

How they slept last night,
the dream that caged them back to back,
was nothing new.

Last words, tears, most often

come wrapped as the everyday
familiar failure.

Now, pulling the comb slowly
through her loosened hair
she tries to find the parting;

it must come out after all:
hidden in all that tangle
there is a way.

1963

Winter

Dead, dead, dead, dead.
A beast of the Middle Ages
stupefied in its den.
The hairs on its body—a woman's—
cold as hairs on a bulb or tuber.

Nothing so bleakly leaden, you tell me,
as the hyacinth's dull cone
before it bulks into blueness.
Ah, but I'd chosen to be
a woman, not a beast or a tuber!

No one knows where the storks went,
everyone knows they have disappeared.
Something—that woman—seems to have
migrated also; if she lives, she lives
sea-zones away, and the meaning grows colder.

1965

Postcard

Rodin's Orpheus, floodlit, hacked,
clawing I don't know what
with the huge toes of an animal,
gripping the air
above the mitered floors
of the Musée . . .

This comes in the mail and I wonder
what it is to be cast in bronze
like the sender;
who wouldn't live, thirsty, drifting,
obscure, freaked-out
but with a future
still lapping at the door
and a dream of language
unlived behind the clouds?

Orpheus hurts all over
but his throat hurts worst of all.
You can see it: the two knobs
of bronze pain in his neck,
the paralysis of his floodlit lips.

1967

The Days: Spring

He writes: *Let us bear
our illusions together* . . .
I persist in thinking:

every fantasy I have
comes true; who am I
to bear illusions?

He writes: *But who can be
a saint?*—The woman in #9
is locked in the bathroom.
She screams for five hours,
pounds the walls, hears voices
retreating in the hall.
The lock is broken.
The lovers pass and go out to lunch,
boredom sets in by 2 o'clock.

Emptiness of the mirror and
the failure of the classics.
A look at the ceiling
in pauses of lovemaking:
that immense, scarred domain.

He writes: *The depth of pain
grows all the time.*
We marched and sat down in the street,
she offered her torn newspaper.
Who will survive Amerika?
they sang on Lenox Avenue.

This early summer weekend.
The chance of beginning again.
From always fewer chances
the future plots itself.
I walk Third Avenue,
bare-armed with flowing hair.
Later the stars come out like facts,
my constellation streams at my head,
a woman's body nailed with stars.

1969

Tear Gas

*(October 12, 1969: reports of the tear-gassing of demonstrators
protesting the treatment of G.I. prisoners in the stockade at
Fort Dix, New Jersey)*

This is how it feels to do something you are afraid of.
That they are afraid of.

> (Would it have been different at Fort Dix, beginning
> to feel the full volume of tears in you, the measure
> of all you have in you to shed, all you have held
> back from false pride, false indifference, false
> courage
>
> beginning to weep as you weep peeling onions, but
> endlessly, for the rest of time, tears of chemistry,
> tears of catalyst, tears of rage, tears for yourself,
> tears for the tortured men in the stockade and for
> their torturers
>
> tears of fear, of the child stepping into the adult
> field of force, the woman stepping into the male field
> of violence, tears of relief, that your body was here,
> you had done it, every last refusal was over)

Here in this house my tears are running wild
in this Vermont of india-madras-colored leaves, of cesspool-
    stricken brooks, of violence licking at old people and
    children
and I am afraid
of the language in my head
I am alone, alone with language
and without meaning
coming back to something written years ago:
our words misunderstand us

wanting a word that will shed itself like a tear
onto the page
leaving its stain

Trying every key in the bunch to get the door even ajar
not knowing whether it's locked or simply jammed from long disuse
trying the keys over and over then throwing the bunch away
staring around for an axe
wondering if the world can be changed like this
if a life can be changed like this

It wasn't completeness I wanted
(the old ideas of a revolution that could be foretold, and once
        arrived at would give us ourselves and each other)
I stopped listening long ago to their descriptions
of the good society

The will to change begins in the body not in the mind
My politics is in my body, accruing and expanding with every
        act of resistance and each of my failures
Locked in the closet at 4 years old I beat the wall with my body
that act is in me still

No, not completeness:
but I needed a way of saying
(this is what they are afraid of)
that could deal with these fragments
I needed to touch you
with a hand, a body
but also with words
I need a language to hear myself with
to see myself in
a language like pigment released on the board
blood-black, sexual green, reds
veined with contradictions
bursting under pressure from the tube
staining the old grain of the wood
like sperm or tears
but this is not what I mean

these images are not what I mean
(I am afraid.)
I mean that I want you to answer me
when I speak badly
that I love you, that we are in danger
that she wants to have your child, that I want us to have mercy
   on each other
that I want to take her hand
that I see you changing
that it was change I loved in you
when I thought I loved completeness
that things I have said which in a few years will be forgotten
matter more to me than this or any poem
and I want you to listen
when I speak badly
not in poems but in tears
not my best but my worst
that these repetitions are beating their way
toward a place where we can no longer be together
where my body no longer will demonstrate outside your stockade
and wheeling through its blind tears will make for the open air
of another kind of action

(I am afraid.)
It's not the worst way to live.

1969

From

The Will to Change

1971

November 1968

Stripped
you're beginning to float free
up through the smoke of brushfires
and incinerators
the unleafed branches won't hold you
nor the radar aerials

You're what the autumn knew would happen
after the last collapse
of primary color
once the last absolutes were torn to pieces
you could begin

How you broke open, what sheathed you
until this moment
I know nothing about it
my ignorance of you amazes me
now that I watch you
starting to give yourself away
to the wind

1968

Study of History

Out there.   The mind of the river
as it might be you.

Lights   blotted by unseen hulls
repetitive shapes passing
dull foam crusting the margin

145

barges sunk below the water-line with silence.
The scow, drudging on.

Lying in the dark, to think of you
and your harsh traffic
gulls pecking your rubbish   natural historians
mourning your lost purity
pleasure cruisers
witlessly careening you

but this
after all
is the narrows and after
all we have never entirely
known what was done to you upstream
what powers trepanned
which of your channels diverted
what rockface leaned to stare
in your upturned
defenseless
face.

1968

Planetarium

Thinking of Caroline Herschel (1750–1848)
astronomer, sister of William; and others.

A woman in the shape of a monster
a monster in the shape of a woman
the skies are full of them

a woman   'in the snow
among the Clocks and instruments
or measuring the ground with poles'

in her 98 years to discover
8 comets

she whom the moon ruled
like us
levitating into the night sky
riding the polished lenses

Galaxies of women, there
doing penance for impetuousness
ribs chilled
in those spaces   of the mind

An eye,

      'virile, precise and absolutely certain'
      from the mad webs of Uranusborg

                  encountering the NOVA

every impulse of light exploding
from the core
as life flies out of us

      Tycho whispering at last
      'Let me not seem to have lived in vain'

What we see, we see
and seeing is changing

the light that shrivels a mountain
and leaves a man alive

Heartbeat of the pulsar
heart sweating through my body

The radio impulse
pouring in from Taurus

        I am bombarded yet   I stand

I have been standing all my life in the
direct path of a battery of signals
the most accurately transmitted most
untranslatable language in the universe
I am a galactic cloud so deep   so invo-
luted that a light wave could take 15
years to travel through me   And has
taken   I am an instrument in the shape
of a woman trying to translate pulsations
into images   for the relief of the body
and the reconstruction of the mind.

1968

The Burning of Paper Instead of Children

> *I was in danger of
> verbalizing my moral
> impulses out of existence.*
> —Daniel Berrigan,
> *on trial in Baltimore.*

1. My neighbor, a scientist and art-collector, telephones me in a
state of violent emotion. He tells me that my son and his, aged
eleven and twelve, have on the last day of school burned a mathe-
matics textbook in the backyard. He has forbidden my son to come
to his house for a week, and has forbidden his own son to leave the
house during that time. "The burning of a book," he says, "arouses
terrible sensations in me, memories of Hitler; there are few things
that upset me so much as the idea of burning a book."

Back there: the library, walled
with green Britannicas
Looking again

in Dürer's *Complete Works*
for MELANCOLIA, the baffled woman

the crocodiles in Herodotus
the Book of the Dead
the *Trial of Jeanne d'Arc,* so blue
I think, It is her color

and they take the book away
because I dream of her too often

love and fear in a house
knowledge of the oppressor
I know it hurts to burn

2. To imagine a time of silence
or few words
a time of chemistry and music

the hollows above your buttocks
traced by my hand
or, *hair is like flesh,* you said

an age of long silence

relief

from this tongue   this slab of limestone
or reinforced concrete
fanatics and traders
dumped on this coast wildgreen clayred
that breathed once
in signals of smoke
sweep of the wind

knowledge of the oppressor
this is the oppressor's language

yet I need it to talk to you

3. *People suffer highly in poverty and it takes dignity and intelligence to overcome this suffering. Some of the suffering are: a child did not had dinner last night: a child steal because he did not have money to buy it: to hear a mother say she do not have money to buy food for her children and to see a child without cloth it will make tears in your eyes.*

(the fracture of order
the repair of speech
to overcome this suffering)

4. We lie under the sheet
after making love, speaking
of loneliness
relieved in a book
relived in a book
so on that page
the clot and fissure
of it appears
words of a man
in pain
a naked word
entering the clot
a hand grasping
through bars:

deliverance

What happens between us
has happened for centuries
we know it from literature

still it happens

sexual jealousy
outflung hand
beating bed

dryness of mouth
after panting

there are books that describe all this
and they are useless

You walk into the woods behind a house
there in that country
you find a temple
built eighteen hundred years ago
you enter without knowing
what it is you enter

so it is with us

no one knows what may happen
though the books tell everything

burn the texts   said Artaud

5. I am composing on the typewriter late at night, thinking of
today. How well we all spoke. A language is a map of our failures.
Frederick Douglass wrote an English purer than Milton's. People
suffer highly in poverty. There are methods but we do not use them.
Joan, who could not read, spoke some peasant form of French.
Some of the suffering are: it is hard to tell the truth; this is America;
I cannot touch you now. In America we have only the present tense.
I am in danger. You are in danger. The burning of a book arouses
no sensation in me. I know it hurts to burn. There are flames of
napalm in Catonsville, Maryland. I know it hurts to burn. The
typewriter is overheated, my mouth is burning, I cannot touch you
and this is the oppressor's language.

1968

I Dream I'm the Death of Orpheus

I am walking rapidly through striations of light and dark thrown
     under an arcade.

I am a woman in the prime of life, with certain powers
and those powers severely limited

by authorities whose faces I rarely see.
I am a woman in the prime of life
driving her dead poet in a black Rolls-Royce
through a landscape of twilight and thorns.
A woman with a certain mission
which if obeyed to the letter will leave her intact.
A woman with the nerves of a panther
a woman with contacts among Hell's Angels
a woman feeling the fullness of her powers
at the precise moment when she must not use them
a woman sworn to lucidity
who sees through the mayhem, the smoky fires
of these underground streets
her dead poet learning to walk backward against the wind
on the wrong side of the mirror

1968

The Blue Ghazals

9/21/68

Violently asleep in the old house.
A clock stays awake all night ticking.

Turning, turning their bruised leaves
the trees stay awake all night in the wood.

Talk to me with your body through my dreams.
Tell me what we are going through.

The walls of the room are muttering,
old trees, old Utopians, arguing with the wind.

To float like a dead man in a sea of dreams
and half those dreams being dreamed by someone else.

Fifteen years of sleepwalking with you,
wading against the tide, and with the tide.

9/23/68

One day of equinoctial light after another,
moving ourselves through gauzes and fissures of that light.

Early and late I come and set myself against you,
your phallic fist knocking blindly at my door.

The dew is beaded like mercury on the coarsened grass,
the web of the spider is heavy as if with sweat.

Everything is yielding toward a foregone conclusion,
only we are rash enough to go on changing our lives.

An Ashanti woman tilts the flattened basin on her head
to let the water slide downward: I am that woman
        and that water.

9/28/68

A man, a woman, a city.
The city as object of love.

Anger and filth in the basement.
The furnace stoked and blazing.

A sexual heat on the pavements.
Trees erected like statues.

Eyes at the ends of avenues.
Yellow for hesitation.

I'm tired of walking your streets
he says, unable to leave her.

Air of dust and rising sparks,
the city burning her letters.

12/13/68

They say, if you can tell, clasped tight under the blanket,
the edge of dark from the edge of dawn, your love is a lie.

If I thought of my words as changing minds,
hadn't my mind also to suffer changes?

They measure fever, swab the blisters of the throat,
but the cells of thought go rioting on ignored.

It's the inner ghost that suffers, little spirit
looking out wildly from the clouded pupils.

When will we lie clearheaded in our flesh again
with the cold edge of the night driving us close together?

12/20/68: i

There are days when I seem to have nothing
but these frayed packets, done up with rotting thread.

The shortest day of the year, let it be ours.
Let me give you something: a token for the subway.

(Refuse even
the most beloved old solutions.

That dead man wrote, grief ought to reach the lips.
You must believe I know before you can tell me.

A black run through the tunnelled winter, he and she,
together, touching, yet not side by side.

12/20/68: ii

Frost, burning. The city's ill.
We gather like viruses.

The doctors are all on their yachts
watching the beautiful skin-divers.

The peasant mind of the Christian
transfixed on food at the year's turning.

Thinking of marzipan
forget that revolutionary child.

Thought grown senile with sweetness.
You too may visit the Virgins.

In the clear air, hijacked planes
touch down at the forbidden island.

5/4/69

Pain made her conservative.
Where the matches touched her flesh, she wears a scar.

The police arrive at dawn
like death and childbirth.

City of accidents, your true map
is the tangling of all our lifelines.

The moment when a feeling enters the body
is political. This touch is political.

Sometimes I dream we are floating on water
hand-in-hand; and sinking without terror.

Pierrot Le Fou

1.

Suppose you stood facing
a wall
      of photographs
from your unlived life

as you stand looking at these
stills from the unseen film?

Yourself against a wall
curiously stuccoed

Yourself in the doorway
of a kind of watchman's hut

Yourself at a window
signalling to people
you haven't met yet

Yourself in unfamiliar clothes
with the same eyes

2.

On a screen as wide as this, I grope for the titles.
I speak the French language like a schoolgirl of the 'forties.
Those roads remind me of Beauce and the motorcycle.
We rode from Paris to Chartres in the March wind.
He said we should go to Spain but the wind defeated me.
France of the superhighways, I never knew you.
How much the body took in those days, and could take!
A naked lightbulb still simmers in my eyeballs.
In every hotel, I lived on the top floor.

3.

Suppose we had time
and no money
living by our wits
                telling stories

which stories would you tell?

I would tell the story
of Pierrot Le Fou
who trusted
            not a woman
                    but love itself

till his head blew off
not quite intentionally

I would tell all the stories I knew
in which people went wrong
but the nervous system

was right all along

4.

The island blistered our feet.
At first we mispronounced each others' names.
All the leaves of the tree were scribbled with words.
There was a language there but no-one to speak it.
Sometimes each of us was alone.
At noon on the beach our shadows left us.
The net we twisted from memory kept on breaking.
The damaged canoe lay on the beach like a dead animal.
You started keeping a journal on a coconut shell.

5.

When I close my eyes
other films
          have been there all along—

a market shot:
bins of turnips, feet
of dead chickens
close-up: a black old woman
buying voodoo medicines

a figure of terrible faith
and I know her needs

Another film:
          an empty room stacked with old films
I am kneeling on the floor
it is getting dark
          they want to close the building
and I still haven't found you

Scanning reel after reel
tundras in negative,
the Bowery
              all those scenes

but the light is failing
                        and you are missing
from the footage of the march
the railway disaster
the snowbound village

even the shots of the island
miss you
              yet you were there

6.

To record
in order to see

                        if you know how the story ends
                        why tell it

To record
in order to forget

                        the surface is always lucid
                        my shadows are under the skin

To record
in order to control

                        the eye of the camera
                        doesn't weep tears of blood

To record
for that is what one does

                        climbing your stairs, over and over
                        I memorized the bare walls

                        This is my way of coming back

1969

Letters: March 1969

1.

Foreknown. The victor
sees the disaster through and through.
His soles grind rocksalt
from roads of the resistance.
He shoulders through rows
of armored faces
he might have loved and lived among.
The victory carried like a corpse
from town to town
begins to crawl in the casket.
The summer swindled on
from town to town, our train
stopping and broiling on the rails
long enough to let on who we were.
The disaster sat up with us all night
drinking bottled water, eating fruit,
talking of the conditions that prevailed.
Outside along the railroad cut
they were singing for our death.

2.

Hopes sparkle like water in the clean carafe.
How little it takes
to restore composure.
White napkins, a tray
of napoleons and cherry tarts
compliments of the airline
which has flown us out of danger.
They are torturing the journalist we drank with
last night in the lounge
but we can't be sure of that

here overlooking the runway
three hours and twenty minutes into another life.
If this is done for us
(and this is done for us)
if we are well men wearing bandages
for disguise
if we can choose our scene
stay out of earshot
break the roll and pour
from the clean carafe
if we can desert like soldiers
abjure like thieves
we may well purchase new virtues at the gate
of the other world.

3.

"I am up at sunrise
collecting data.
The reservoir burns green.
Darling, the knives they have on this block alone
would amaze you.
When they ask my profession I say
I'm a student of weapons systems.
The notes I'm putting together are purely
of sentimental value
my briefcase is I swear useless
to foreign powers, to the police
I am not given I say
to revealing my sources
to handing round copies
of my dossier for perusal.
The vulnerable go unarmed.
I myself walk the floor
a ruinously expensive Swiss hunting knife
exposed in my brain
eight blades, each one for a distinct purpose,
laid open as on the desk
of an importer or a fence."

4.

Six months back
send carbons you said
but this winter's dashed off in pencil
torn off the pad too fast
for those skills. In the dawn taxi
in the kitchen
burning the succotash
the more I love my life the more
I love you. In a time
of fear. In a city
of fears. In a life
without vacations the paisley fades
winter and summer in the sun
but the best time is now.

My sick friend writes: *what's love?*
This life is nothing, Adrienne!

Her hands bled onto the sill.
She had that trick of reaching outward,
the pane was smashed but only
the calvinist northwind
spat in from the sea.
She's a shot hero. A dying poet.
Even now, if we went for her—
but they've gone with rags and putty to fix the pane.
She stays in with her mirrors and anger.

I tear up answers
I once gave, postcards
from riot and famine go up on the walls
valentines stuck in the mirror
flame and curl, loyalties dwindle
the bleak light dries our tears
without relief. I keep coming back to you

in my head, but you couldn't know that, and
I have no carbons. Prince of pity,

what eats out of your hand?
the rodent pain, electric
with exhaustion, mazed and shaken?
I'd have sucked the wound in your hand to sleep
but my lips were trembling.
Tell me how to bear myself,
how it's done, the light kiss falling
accurately
on the cracked palm.

1969

Pieces

1. *Breakpoint*

The music of words
received as fact

The steps that wouldn't hold us both
splintering in air.

The self witheld in an urn
like ashes

To have loved you better than you loved yourself
—whoever you were, to have loved you—

And still to love but simply
as one of those faces on the street

2. *Relevance*

That erudition
how to confront it

The critics wrote answers
the questions were ours

A breast, a shoulder
chilled at waking

The cup of yogurt
eaten at noon
and no explanations

The books we borrowed
trying to read each other's minds

Paperbacks piling
on both sides of the fireplace
and piled beside the bed

What difference could it make
that those books came
out of unintelligible pain

as daylight out of the hours

when that light burned
atop the insurance tower
all night like the moon

3. *Memory*

Plugged-in to her body
he came the whole way
but it makes no difference

If not this then what
would fuse a connection

(All that burning intelligence about love
what can it matter

Falling in love on words
and ending in silence
with its double-meanings

Always falling and ending
because this world gives no room
to be what we dreamt of being

Are we, as he said
of the generation that forgets
the lightning-flash, the air-raid

and each other

4. *Time and Place*

Liquid mist burning off
along the highway

Slap of water
Light on shack boards

Hauling of garbage
early in the wet street

Always the same, wherever waking,
the old positions
assumed by the mind

and the new day forms
like a china cup

hard, cream-colored, unbreakable
even in our travels

5. *Revelation*

This morning: read Simone Weil
on the loss of grace

drank a glass of water

remembered the dream that woke me:

some one, some more than one
battering into my room
intent to kill me

I crying your name
its two syllables
ringing through sleep

knowing it vain
knowing
you slept unhearing

crying your name
like a spell

like signs executed

by the superstitious

who are the faithful of this world

1969

Our Whole Life

Our whole life a translation
the permissible fibs

and now a knot of lies
eating at itself to get undone

Words bitten thru words

meanings burnt-off like paint
under the blowtorch

All those dead letters
rendered into the oppressor's language

Trying to tell the doctor where it hurts
like the Algerian
who walked from his village, burning

his whole body a cloud of pain
and there are no words for this

except himself

1969

STAND UP in my nightgown at the window
almost naked behind black glass

Off from the line of trees the road
beaten, bare, we walked

in the light of the bare, beaten moon.
Almost, you spoke to me. The road

swings past swampground
the soft spots of the earth

you might sink through into location
where their cameras are set up

the underground film-makers waiting to make their film
waiting for you

their cameras pivot toward your head and the film burns
but you're not talking

If I am there you have forgotten my name
you think perhaps: *a woman*

and you drift on, drifter, through the frames
of the movie they are making of this time.

A whole soundtrack of your silence
a whole film

of dark nights and darker rooms
and blank sheets of paper, bare . . .

1969

The Photograph of the Unmade Bed

Cruelty is rarely conscious
One slip of the tongue

one exposure
among so many

a thrust in the dark
to see if there's pain there

I never asked you to explain
that act of violence

what dazed me was our ignorance
of our will to hurt each other

. . . . . .

In a flash I understand
how poems are unlike photographs

(the one saying   *This could be*
the other   *This was*

The image
isn't responsible

for our uses of it
It is intentionless

A long strand of dark hair
in the washbasin

is innocent and yet
such things have done harm

. . . . . .

These snapshots taken by ghetto children
given for Christmas

Objects blurring into perceptions
No 'art,' only the faults

of the film, the faults of the time
Did mere indifference blister

these panes, eat these walls,
shrivel and scrub these trees—

mere indifference? I tell you
cruelty is rarely conscious

the done and the undone blur
into one photograph of failure

. . . . . .

This crust of bread we try to share
this name traced on a window

this word I paste together
like a child fumbling

with paste and scissors
this writing in the sky with smoke

this silence

this lettering chalked on the ruins
this alphabet of the dumb

this feather held to lips
that still breathe and are warm

1969

Images for Godard

1. Language as city:: Wittgenstein:
   Driving to the limits
   of the city of words

   the superhighway streams
   like a comic strip

   to newer suburbs
   casements of shockproof glass

   where no one yet looks out
   or toward the coast where even now

   the squatters in their shacks
   await eviction

When all conversation
becomes an interview
under duress

when we come to the limits
of the city

my face must have a meaning

2. To know the extremes of light
I sit in this darkness

To see the present flashing
in a rearview mirror

blued in a plateglass pane
reddened in the reflection

of the red Triomphe
parked at the edge of the sea

the sea glittering in the sun
the swirls of nebula

in the espresso cup
raindrops, neon spectra

on a vinyl raincoat

3. To love, to move perpetually
as the body changes

a dozen times a day
the temperature of the skin

the feeling of rise & fall
deadweight & buoyancy

the eye sunk inward
the eye bleeding with speech

for that moment at least
I wás you—

To be stopped, to shoot the same scene
over & over

4. At the end of *Alphaville*
she says *I love you*

and the film begins
that you've said you'd never make

because it's impossible:
things as difficult to show
as horror & war & sickness are

meaning: *love,*
to speak in the mouth

to touch the breast
for a woman

to know the sex of a man
That film begins here

yet you don't show it
we leave the theatre

suffering from that

5. Interior monologue of the poet:
the notes for the poem are the only poem

the mind collecting, devouring
all these destructibles

the unmade studio couch the air
shifting the abalone shells

the mind of the poet is the only poem
the poet is at the movies

dreaming the film-maker's dream but differently
free in the dark as if asleep

free in the dusty beam of the projector
the mind of the poet is changing

the moment of change is the only poem

1970

A Valediction Forbidding Mourning

My swirling wants. Your frozen lips.
The grammar turned and attacked me.
Themes, written under duress.
Emptiness of the notations.

They gave me a drug that slowed the healing of wounds.

I want you to see this before I leave:
the experience of repetition as death
the failure of criticism to locate the pain
the poster in the bus that said:
my bleeding is under control.

A red plant in a cemetery of plastic wreaths.

A last attempt: the language is a dialect called metaphor.
These images go unglossed: hair, glacier, flashlight.
When I think of a landscape I am thinking of a time.
When I talk of taking a trip I mean forever.
I could say: those mountains have a meaning
but further than that I could not say.

To do something very common, in my own way.

1970

Shooting Script

PART I 11/69–2/70

1.

We were bound on the wheel of an endless conversation.

Inside this shell, a tide waiting for someone to enter.

A monologue waiting for you to interrupt it.

A man wading into the surf. The dialogue of the rock with the breaker.

The wave changed instantly by the rock; the rock changed by the wave returning over and over.

The dialogue that lasts all night or a whole lifetime.

A conversation of sounds melting constantly into rhythms.

A shell waiting for you to listen.

A tide that ebbs and flows against a deserted continent.

A cycle whose rhythm begins to change the meanings of words.

A wheel of blinding waves of light, the spokes pulsing out from where we hang together in the turning of an endless conversation.

The meaning that searches for its word like a hermit crab.

A monologue that waits for one listener.

An ear filled with one sound only.

A shell penetrated by meaning.

2.

Adapted from Mirza Ghalib

Even when I thought I prayed, I was talking to myself; when I
found the door shut, I simply walked away.

We all accept Your claim to be unique; the stone lips, the
carved limbs, were never your true portrait.

Grief held back from the lips wears at the heart; the drop that
refused to join the river dried up in the dust.

Now tell me your story till the blood drips from your lashes. Any
other version belongs to your folklore, or ours.

To see the Tigris in a water-drop . . . Either you were playing
games with me, or you never cared to learn the structure of my
language.

3.

The old blanket. The crumbs of rubbed wool turning up.

Where we lay and breakfasted. The stains of tea. The squares
of winter light projected on the wool.

You, sleeping with closed windows. I, sleeping in the silver
nitrate burn of zero air.

Where it can snow, I'm at home; the crystals accumulating
spell out my story.

The cold encrustation thickening on the ledge.

The arrow-headed facts, accumulating, till a whole city is
taken over.

Midwinter and the loss of love, going comes before gone, over
and over the point is missed and still the blind will turns for
its target.

4.

In my imagination I was the pivot of a fresh beginning.

In rafts they came over the sea; on the island they put up those stones by methods we can only guess at.

If the vegetation grows as thick as this, how can we see what they were seeing?

It is all being made clear, with bulldozers, at Angkor Wat.

The verdure was a false mystery; the baring of the stones is no solution for us now.

Defoliation progresses; concrete is poured, sheets of glass hauled overland in huge trucks and at great cost.

Here we never travailed, never took off our shoes to walk the final mile.

Come and look into this cellar-hole; this is the foundling of the woods.

Humans lived here once; it became sacred only when they went away.

5.

Of simple choice they are the villagers; their clothes come with them like red clay roads they have been walking.

The sole of the foot is a map, the palm of the hand a letter, learned by heart and worn close to the body.

They seemed strange to me, till I began to recall their dialect.

Poking the spade into the dry loam, listening for the tick of broken pottery, hoarding the brown and black bits in a dented can.

Evenings, at the table, turning the findings out, pushing them
around with a finger, beginning to dream of fitting them together.

Hiding all this work from them, although they might have helped
me.

Going up at night, hiding the tin can in a closet, where the linoleum
lies in shatters on a back shelf.

Sleeping to dream of the unformed, the veil of water pouring over
the wet clay, the rhythms of choice, the lost methods.

6.

You are beside me like a wall; I touch you with my fingers and
keep moving through the bad light.

At this time of year when faces turn aside, it is amazing that your
eyes are to be met.

A bad light is one like this, that flickers and diffuses itself along
the edge of a frontier.

No, I don't invest you with anything; I am counting on your
weakness as much as on your strength.

This light eats away at the clarities I had fixed on; it moves up
like a rodent at the edge of the raked paths.

Your clarities may not reach me; but your attention will.

It is to know that I too have no mythic powers; it is to see the
liability of all my treasures.

You will have to see all this for a long time alone.

You are beside me like a wall; I touch you with my fingers and
keep trying to move through the bad light.

7.

Picking the wax to crumbs in the iron lip of the candelabrum.

Fingering down the thread of the maze where the green strand cuts
across the violet strand.

Picking apart the strands of pain; a warp of wool dipped in burning
wax.

When the flame shrinks to a blue bead, there is danger; the change
of light in a flickering situation.

Stretched on the loom the light expands; the smell of a smell of
burning.

When the change leaves you dark, when the wax cools in the socket,
when I thought I prayed, when I was talking to myself under the
cover of my darkness.

Someone who never said, "What do you feel?" someone who sat
across from me, taking the crumbs of wax as I picked them apart
and handed them over.

PART II 3–7/70

8.

—for Hugh Seidman

A woman waking behind grimed blinds slatted across a courtyard
she never looks into.

Thinking of the force of a waterfall, the slash of cold air from the
thickest water of the falls, slicing the green and ochre afternoon
in which he turns his head and walks away.

Thinking of that place as an existence.

A woman reaching for the glass of water left all night on the bureau,
the half-done poem, the immediate relief.

Entering the poem as a method of leaving the room.

Entering the paper airplane of the poem, which somewhere before
its destination starts curling into ash and comes apart.

The woman is too heavy for the poem, she is a swollenness, a foot,
an arm, gone asleep, grown absurd and out of bounds.

Rooted to memory like a wedge in a block of wood; she takes the
pressure of her thought but cannot resist it.

You call this a poetry of false problems, the shotgun wedding of the
mind, the subversion of choice by language.

Instead of the alternative: to pull the sooty strings to set the
window bare to purge the room with light to feel the sun breaking
in on the courtyard and the steamheat smothering in the shut-off
pipes.

To feel existence as this time, this place, the pathos and force
of the lumps of snow gritted and melting in the unloved corners of
the courtyard.

9.
NEWSREEL

This would not be the war we fought in. See, the foliage is
heavier, there were no hills of that size there.

But I find it impossible not to look for actual persons known
to me and not seen since; impossible not to look for myself.

The scenery angers me, I know there is something wrong, the sun
is too high, the grass too trampled, the peasants' faces too broad,
and the main square of the capital had no arcades like those.

Yet the dead look right, and the roofs of the huts, and the crashed
fuselage burning among the ferns.

But this is not the war I came to see, buying my ticket, stumbling through the darkness, finding my place among the sleepers and masturbators in the dark.

I thought of seeing the General who cursed us, whose name they gave to an expressway; I wanted to see the faces of the dead when they were living.

Once I know they filmed us, back at the camp behind the lines, taking showers under the trees and showing pictures of our girls.

Somewhere there is a film of the war we fought in, and it must contain the flares, the souvenirs, the shadows of the netted brush, the standing in line of the innocent, the hills that were not of this size.

Somewhere my body goes taut under the deluge, somewhere I am naked behind the lines, washing my body in the water of that war.

Someone has that war stored up in metal canisters, a memory he cannot use, somewhere my innocence is proven with my guilt, but this would not be the war I fought in.

10.

—*for Valerie Glauber*

They come to you with their descriptions of your soul.

They come and drop their mementos at the foot of your bed; their feathers, ferns, fans, grasses from the western mountains.

They wait for you to unfold for them like a paper flower, a secret springing open in a glass of water.

They believe your future has a history and that it is themselves.

They have family trees to plant for you, photographs of dead children, old bracelets and rings they want to fasten onto you.

And, in spite of this, you live alone.

Your secret hangs in the open like Poe's purloined letter; their longing and their methods will never let them find it.

Your secret cries out in the dark and hushes; when they start out of sleep they think you are innocent.

You hang among them like the icon in a Russian play; living your own intenser life behind the lamp they light in front of you.

You are spilt here like mercury on a marble counter, liquefying into many globes, each silvered like a planet caught in a lens.

You are a mirror lost in a brook, an eye reflecting a torrent of reflections.

You are a letter written, folded, burnt to ash, and mailed in an envelope to another continent.

11.

The mare's skeleton in the clearing: another sign of life.

When you pull the embedded bones up from the soil, the flies collect again.

The pelvis, the open archway, staring at me like an eye.

In the desert these bones would be burnt white; a green bloom grows on them in the woods.

Did she break her leg or die of poison?

What was it like when the scavengers came?

So many questions unanswered, yet the statement is here and clear.

With what joy you handled the skull, set back the teeth spilt in the grass, hinged back the jaw on the jaw.

With what joy we left the woods, swinging our sticks, miming the
speech of noble savages, of the fathers of our country, bursting
into the full sun of the uncut field.

12.

I was looking for a way out of a lifetime's consolations.

We walked in the wholesale district: closed warehouses, windows,
steeped in sun.

I said: those cloths are very old. You said: they have lain in
that window a long time.

When the skeletons of the projects shut off the sunset, when the
sense of the Hudson leaves us, when only by loss of light in the east
do I know that I am living in the west.

When I give up being paraphrased, when I let go, when the
beautiful solutions in their crystal flasks have dried up in the sun,
when the lightbulb bursts on lighting, when the dead bulb rattles
like a seed-pod.

Those cloths are very old, they are mummies' cloths, they have lain
in graves, they were not intended to be sold, the tragedy of this
mistake will soon be clear.

Vacillant needles of Manhattan, describing hour & weather; buying
these descriptions at the cost of missing every other point.

13.

We are driven to odd attempts; once it would not have occurred to
me to put out in a boat, not on a night like this.

Still, it was an instrument, and I had pledged myself to try any
instrument that came my way. Never to refuse one from conviction
of incompetence.

A long time I was simply learning to handle the skiff; I had no
special training and my own training was against me.

I had always heard that darkness and water were a threat.

In spite of this, darkness and water helped me to arrive here.

I watched the lights on the shore I had left for a long time; each
one, it seemed to me, was a light I might have lit, in the old days.

14.

Whatever it was: the grains of the glacier caked in the boot-cleats;
ashes spilled on white formica.

The death-col viewed through power-glasses; the cube of ice melting
on stainless steel.

Whatever it was, the image that stopped you, the one on which you
came to grief, projecting it over & over on empty walls.

Now to give up the temptations of the projector; to see instead the
web of cracks filtering across the plaster.

To read there the map of the future, the roads radiating from the
initial split, the filaments thrown out from that impasse.

To reread the instructions on your palm; to find there how the
lifeline, broken, keeps its direction.

To read the etched rays of the bullet-hole left years ago in the
glass; to know in every distortion of the light what fracture is.

To put the prism in your pocket, the thin glass lens, the map
of the inner city, the little book with gridded pages.

To pull yourself up by your own roots; to eat the last meal in
your old neighborhood.

From

Diving into the Wreck

1973

Trying to Talk with a Man

Out in this desert we are testing bombs,

that's why we came here.

Sometimes I feel an underground river
forcing its way between deformed cliffs
an acute angle of understanding
moving itself like a locus of the sun
into this condemned scenery.

What we've had to give up to get here—
whole LP collections, films we starred in
playing in the neighborhoods, bakery windows
full of dry, chocolate-filled Jewish cookies,
the language of love-letters, of suicide notes,
afternoons on the riverbank
pretending to be children

Coming out to this desert
we meant to change the face of
driving among dull green succulents
walking at noon in the ghost town
surrounded by a silence

that sounds like the silence of the place
except that it came with us
and is familiar
and everything we were saying until now
was an effort to blot it out—
coming out here we are up against it

Out here I feel more helpless
with you than without you

You mention the danger
and list the equipment
we talk of people caring for each other
in emergencies—laceration, thirst—
but you look at me like an emergency

Your dry heat feels like power
your eyes are stars of a different magnitude
they reflect lights that spell out: EXIT
when you get up and pace the floor

talking of the danger
as if it were not ourselves
as if we were testing anything else.

1971

When We Dead Awaken

—for E.Y.

Trying to tell you how
the anatomy of the park
through stained panes, the way
guerrillas are advancing
through minefields, the trash
burning endlessly in the dump
to return to heaven like a stain—
everything outside our skins is an image
of this affliction:
stones on my table, carried by hand
from scenes I trusted
souvenirs of what I once described
as happiness
everything outside my skin
speaks of the fault that sends me limping
even the scars of my decisions

even the sunblaze in the mica-vein
even you, fellow-creature, sister,
sitting across from me, dark with love,
working like me to pick apart
working with me to remake
this trailing knitted thing, this cloth of darkness,
this woman's garment, trying to save the skein.

2.

The fact of being separate
enters your livelihood like a piece of furniture
—a chest of seventeenth-century wood
from somewhere in the North.
It has a huge lock shaped like a woman's head
but the key has not been found.
In the compartments are other keys
to lost doors, an eye of glass.
Slowly you begin to add
things of your own.
You come and go reflected in its panels.
You give up keeping track of anniversaries,
you begin to write in your diaries
more honestly than ever.

3.

The lovely landscape of southern Ohio
betrayed by strip mining, the
thick gold band on the adulterer's finger
the blurred programs of the offshore pirate station
are causes for hesitation.
Here in the matrix of need and anger, the
disproof of what we thought possible
failures of medication
doubts of another's existence
—tell it over and over, the words
get thick with unmeaning—
yet never have we been closer to the truth
of the lies we were living, listen to me:

the faithfulness I can imagine would be a weed
flowering in tar, a blue energy piercing
the massed atoms of a bedrock disbelief.

1971

Waking in the Dark

1.

The thing that arrests me is
     how we are composed of molecules

       (he showed me the figure in the paving stones)

     arranged without our knowledge and consent

        like the wirephoto composed
        of millions of dots

        in which the man from Bangladesh
        walks starving
              on the front page
              knowing nothing about it

        which is his presence for the world

2.

We were standing in line outside of something
two by two, or alone in pairs, or simply alone,
looking into windows full of scissors,
windows full of shoes. The street was closing,
the city was closing, would we be the lucky ones
to make it? They were showing
in a glass case, the Man Without A Country.
We held up our passports in his face, we wept for him.

They are dumping animal blood into the sea
to bring up the sharks. Sometimes every

aperture of my body
leaks blood. I don't know whether
to pretend that this is natural.
Is there a law about this, a law of nature?
You worship the blood
you call it hysterical bleeding
you want to drink it like milk
you dip your finger into it and write
you faint at the smell of it
you dream of dumping me into the sea.

3.

The tragedy of sex
lies around us, a woodlot
the axes are sharpened for.
The old shelters and huts
stare through the clearing with a certain resolution
—the hermit's cabin, the hunters' shack—
scenes of masturbation
and dirty jokes.
A man's world. But finished.
They themselves have sold it to the machines.
I walk the unconscious forest,
a woman dressed in old army fatigues
that have shrunk to fit her, I am lost
at moments, I feel dazed
by the sun pawing between the trees,
cold in the bog and lichen of the thicket.
Nothing will save this. I am alone,
kicking the last rotting logs
with their strange smell of life, not death,
wondering what on earth it all might have become.

4.

Clarity,
        spray
blinding and purging

spears of sun striking the water

the bodies riding the air

like gliders

the bodies in slow motion

falling
into the pool
at the Berlin Olympics

control; loss of control

the bodies rising
arching back to the tower
time reeling backward

clarity of open air
before the dark chambers
with the shower-heads

the bodies falling again
freely

                      faster than light
the water opening
like air
like realization

A woman made this film
against

the law
of gravity

5.

All night dreaming of a body
space weighs on differently from mine
We are making love in the street
the traffic flows off from us
pouring back like a sheet
the asphalt stirs with tenderness

there is no dismay
we move together like underwater plants

Over and over, starting to wake
I dive back to discover you
still whispering, *touch me,* we go on
streaming through the slow
citylight forest ocean
stirring our body hair

But this is the saying of a dream
on waking
I wish there were somewhere
actual we could stand
handing the power-glasses back and forth
looking at the earth, the wildwood
where the split began

1971

Incipience

1. To live, to lie awake
under scarred plaster
while ice is forming over the earth
at an hour when nothing can be done
to further any decision

to know the composing of the thread
inside the spider's body
first atoms of the web
visible tomorrow

to feel the fiery future
of every matchstick in the kitchen

Nothing can be done
but by inches. I write out my life
hour by hour, word by word
gazing into the anger of old women on the bus
numbering the striations
of air inside the ice cube
imagining the existence
of something uncreated
this poem
our lives

2. A man is asleep in the next room
        We are his dreams
        We have the heads and breasts of women
        the bodies of birds of prey
        Sometimes we turn into silver serpents
While we sit up smoking and talking of how to live
he turns on the bed and murmurs

A man is asleep in the next room
        A neurosurgeon enters his dream
        and begins to dissect his brain
        She does not look like a nurse
        she is absorbed in her work
        she has a stern, delicate face like Marie Curie
She is not/might be either of us

A man is asleep in the next room
        He has spent a whole day
        standing, throwing stones into the black pool
        which keeps its blackness
Outside the frame of his dream we are stumbling up the hill
        hand in hand, stumbling and guiding each other
        over the scarred volcanic rock

1971

The Mirror in Which
Two Are Seen as One

1.

She is the one you call sister.
Her simplest act has glamor,
as when she scales a fish the knife
flashes in her long fingers
no motion wasted or when
rapidly talking of love
she steel-wool burnishes
the battered kettle

Love apples cramp you sideways
with sudden emptiness
the cereals glutting you, the grains
ripe clusters picked by hand
Love: the refrigerator
with open door
the ripe steaks bleeding
their hearts out in plastic film
the whipped butter, the apricots
the sour leftovers

A crate is waiting in the orchard
for you to fill it
your hands are raw with scraping
the sharp bark, the thorns
of this succulent tree
Pick, pick, pick
this harvest is a failure
the juice runs down your cheekbones
like sweat or tears

2.

She is the one you call sister
you blaze like lightning about the room
flicker around her like fire
dazzle yourself in her wide eyes
listing her unfelt needs
thrusting the tenets of your life
into her hands

natural
active

She moves through a world of India print
her body dappled
with softness, the paisley swells at her hip
walking the street in her cotton shift
buying fresh figs because you love them
photographing the ghetto because you took her there

Why are you crying dry up your tears
we are sisters
words fail you in the stare of her hunger
control
you hand her another book
scored by your pencil
you hand her a record
of two flutes in India reciting

3.

Late summer night the insects
fry in the yellowed lightglobe
your skin burns gold in its light
In this mirror, who are you? Dreams of the nunnery
with its discipline, the nursery
person as object plasticized
with its nurse, the hospital
where all the powerful ones are masked
the graveyard where you sit on the graves
of women who died in childbirth
and women who died at birth
Dreams of your sister's birth
your mother dying in childbirth over and over

not knowing how to stop
bearing you over and over

your mother dead and you unborn
your two hands grasping your head
drawing it down against the blade of life
your nerves the nerves of a midwife
learning her trade

1971

[handwritten marginalia: re-birth of self must be effected by self exploration - growth learning process]

[handwritten marginalia: situations in which women are in control compared to situation in which they are not]

Dialogue

She sits with one hand poised against her head, the
other turning an old ring to the light
for hours our talk has beaten
like rain against the screens
a sense of August and heat-lightning
I get up, go to make tea, come back
we look at each other
then she says (and this is what I live through
over and over)—she says: *I do not know*
if sex is an illusion

I do not know
who I was when I did those things
or who I said I was
or whether I willed to feel
what I had read about
or who in fact was there with me
or whether I knew, even then
that there was doubt about these things

1972

Diving into the Wreck

First having read the book of myths,
and loaded the camera,
and checked the edge of the knife-blade,
I put on
the body-armor of black rubber
the absurd flippers
the grave and awkward mask.
I am having to do this
not like Cousteau with his
assiduous team
aboard the sun-flooded schooner
but here alone.

There is a ladder.
The ladder is always there
hanging innocently
close to the side of the schooner.
We know what it is for,
we who have used it.
Otherwise
it's a piece of maritime floss
some sundry equipment.

I go down.
Rung after rung and still
the oxygen immerses me
the blue light
the clear atoms
of our human air.
I go down.
My flippers cripple me,
I crawl like an insect down the ladder
and there is no one

to tell me when the ocean
will begin.

First the air is blue and then
it is bluer and then green and then
black I am blacking out and yet
my mask is powerful
it pumps my blood with power
the sea is another story
the sea is not a question of power
I have to learn alone
to turn my body without force
in the deep element.

And now: it is easy to forget
what I came for
among so many who have always
lived here
swaying their crenellated fans
between the reefs
and besides
you breathe differently down here.

I came to explore the wreck.
The words are purposes.
The words are maps.
I came to see the damage that was done
and the treasures that prevail.
I stroke the beam of my lamp
slowly along the flank
of something more permanent
than fish or weed

the thing I came for:
the wreck and not the story of the wreck
the thing itself and not the myth
the drowned face always staring
toward the sun
the evidence of damage

worn by salt and sway into this threadbare beauty
the ribs of the disaster
curving their assertion
among the tentative haunters.

This is the place.
And I am here, the mermaid whose dark hair
streams black, the merman in his armored body
We circle silently
about the wreck
we dive into the hold.
I am she: I am he

whose drowned face sleeps with open eyes
whose breasts still bear the stress
whose silver, copper, vermeil cargo lies
obscurely inside barrels
half-wedged and left to rot
we are the half-destroyed instruments
that once held to a course
the water-eaten log
the fouled compass

We are, I am, you are
by cowardice or courage
the one who find our way
back to this scene
carrying a knife, a camera
a book of myths
in which
our names do not appear.

1972

The Phenomenology of Anger

1. The freedom of the wholly mad
to smear & play with her madness

write with her fingers dipped in it
the length of a room

which is not, of course, the freedom
you have, walking on Broadway
to stop & turn back or go on
10 blocks; 20 blocks

but feels enviable maybe
to the compromised

curled in the placenta of the real
which was to feed & which is strangling her.

2. Trying to light a log that's lain in the damp
as long as this house has stood:
even with dry sticks I can't get started
even with thorns.
I twist last year into a knot of old headlines
—this rose won't bloom.

How does a pile of rags the machinist wiped his hands on
feel in its cupboard, hour upon hour?
Each day during the heat-wave
they took the temperature of the haymow.
I huddled fugitive
in the warm sweet simmer of the hay

muttering: *Come.*

3. Flat heartland of winter.
The moonmen come back from the moon
the firemen come out of the fire.
Time without a taste: time without decisions.

Self-hatred, a monotone in the mind.
The shallowness of a life lived in exile
even in the hot countries.
Cleaver, staring into a window full of knives.

4. White light splits the room.
Table. Window. Lampshade. You.

My hands, sticky in a new way.
Menstrual blood
seeming to leak from your side.

Will the judges try to tell me
which was the blood of whom?

5. Madness. Suicide. Murder.
Is there no way out but these?
The enemy, always just out of sight
snowshoeing the next forest, shrouded
in a snowy blur, abominable snowman
—at once the most destructive
and the most elusive being
gunning down the babies at My Lai
vanishing in the face of confrontation.

The prince of air and darkness
computing body counts, masturbating
in the factory
of facts.

6. Fantasies of murder: not enough:
to kill is to cut off from pain
but the killer goes on hurting

Not enough. When I dream of meeting
the enemy, this is my dream:

white acetylene
ripples from my body
effortlessly released
perfectly trained
on the true enemy

raking his body down to the thread
of existence
burning away his lie
leaving him in a new
world; a changed
man

7. I suddenly see the world
as no longer viable:
you are out there burning the crops
with some new sublimate
This morning you left the bed
we still share
and went out to spread impotence
upon the world

I hate you.
I hate the mask you wear, your eyes
assuming a depth
they do not possess, drawing me
into the grotto of your skull
the landscape of bone
I hate your words
they make me think of fake
revolutionary bills
crisp imitation parchment
they sell at battlefields.

Last night, in this room, weeping
I asked you: *what are you feeling?*
do you feel anything?

Now in the torsion of your body
as you defoliate the fields we lived from
I have your answer.

8. Dogeared earth. Wormeaten moon.
A pale cross-hatching of silver
lies like a wire screen on the black
water. All these phenomena
are temporary.

I would have loved to live in a world
of women and men gaily
in collusion with green leaves, stalks,
building mineral cities, transparent domes,
little huts of woven grass
each with its own pattern—

a conspiracy to coexist
with the Crab Nebula, the exploding
universe, the Mind—

9. *The only real love I have ever felt*
was for children and other women.
Everything else was lust, pity,
self-hatred, pity, lust.
This is a woman's confession.
Now, look again at the face
of Botticelli's Venus, Kali,
the Judith of Chartres
with her so-called smile.

10. how we are burning up our lives
testimony:
            the subway
            hurtling to Brooklyn
            her head on her knees
            asleep or drugged

la vía del tren subterráneo
es peligrosa

            many sleep
            the whole way
            others sit
            staring holes of fire into the air
            others plan rebellion:
            night after night
            awake in prison, my mind
            licked at the mattress like a flame
            till the cellblock went up roaring

        Thoreau setting fire to the woods

Every act of becoming conscious
(it says here in this book)
is an unnatural act

1972

A Primary Ground

> *It was sympathy he wanted, to be assured*
> *of his genius, first of all, and then to*
> *be taken within the circle of life, warmed and soothed,*
> *to have his sense restored to him,*
> *his barrenness made fertile, and all the rooms*
> *of the house made full of life . . .*
> —*Virginia Woolf,* To the Lighthouse

And this is how you live: a woman, children
protect you from the abyss
you move near, turning on the news
eating Thanksgiving with its pumpkin teeth
drinking the last wine
from the cellar of your wedding

It all seems innocent enough, this sin
of wedlock: you, your wife, your children
leaning across the unfilled plates
passing the salt
down a cloth ironed by a woman
with aching legs
Now they go out to play
in the coarse, rough November air
that smells of soft-coal smoke, the river,
burnt sweet-potato pie.

Sensuality dessicates in words—
risks of the portage, risks of the glacier
never taken
Protection is the genius of your house
the pressure of the steam iron
flattens the linen cloth again
chestnuts puréed with care are dutifully eaten

in every room the furniture reflects you
larger than life, or dwindling

Emptiness
thrust like a batch of letters to the furthest
dark of a drawer . . .
But there is something else:
your wife's twin sister, speechless
is dying in the house
You and your wife take turns
carrying up the trays,
understanding her case, trying to make her understand.

1972

Translations

You show me the poems of some woman
my age, or younger
translated from your language

Certain words occur: *enemy, oven, sorrow*
enough to let me know
she's a woman of my time

obsessed

with Love, our subject:
we've trained it like ivy to our walls
baked it like bread in our ovens
worn it like lead on our ankles
watched it through binoculars as if
it were a helicopter
bringing food to our famine
or the satellite
of a hostile power

I begin to see that woman
doing things: stirring rice
ironing a skirt
typing a manuscript till dawn

trying to make a call
from a phonebooth

The phone rings unanswered
in a man's bedroom
she hears him telling someone else
Never mind. She'll get tired—
hears him telling her story to her sister

who becomes her enemy
and will in her own time
light her own way to sorrow

ignorant of the fact this way of grief
is shared, unnecessary
and political

1972

The Ninth Symphony of Beethoven
Understood at Last as a Sexual Message

A man in terror of impotence
or infertility, not knowing the difference
a man trying to tell something
howling from the climacteric
music of the entirely
isolated soul
yelling at Joy from the tunnel of the ego
music without the ghost
of another person in it, music

trying to tell something the man
does not want out, would keep if he could
gagged and bound and flogged with chords of Joy
where everything is silence and the
beating of a bloody fist upon
a splintered table

1972

Rape

There is a cop who is both prowler and father:
he comes from your block, grew up with your brothers,
had certain ideals.
You hardly know him in his boots and silver badge,
on horseback, one hand touching his gun.

You hardly know him but you have to get to know him:
he has access to machinery that could kill you.
He and his stallion clop like warlords among the trash,
his ideals stand in the air, a frozen cloud
from between his unsmiling lips.

And so, when the time comes, you have to turn to him,
the maniac's sperm still greasing your thighs,
your mind whirling like crazy. You have to confess
to him, you are guilty of the crime
of having been forced.

And you see his blue eyes, the blue eyes of all the family
whom you used to know, grow narrow and glisten,
his hand types out the details
and he wants them all
but the hysteria in your voice pleases him best.

You hardly know him but now he thinks he knows you:
he has taken down your worst moment

on a machine and filed it in a file.
He knows, or thinks he knows, how much you imagined;
he knows, or thinks he knows, what you secretly wanted.

He has access to machinery that could get you put away;
and if, in the sickening light of the precinct,
and if, in the sickening light of the precinct,
your details sound like a portrait of your confessor,
will you swallow, will you deny them, will you lie your way home?

1972

Burning Oneself In

In a bookstore on the East Side
I read a veteran's testimony:

the running down, for no reason,
of an old woman in South Vietnam
by a U.S. Army truck

The heat-wave is over
Lifeless, sunny, the East Side
rests under its awnings

Another summer
The flames go on feeding

and a dull heat permeates the ground
of the mind, the burn has settled in
as if it had no more question

of its right to go on devouring
the rest of a lifetime,
the rest of history

Pieces of information, like this one
blow onto the heap

they keep it fed, whether we will it or not,
another summer, and another
of suffering quietly

in bookstores, in the parks
however we may scream we are
suffering quietly

1972

Burning Oneself Out

—for E.K.

We can look into the stove tonight
as into a mirror, yes,

the serrated log, the yellow-blue
gaseous core

the crimson-flittered grey ash, yes,
I know inside my eyelids
and underneath my skin

Time takes hold of us like a draft
upward, drawing at the heats
in the belly, in the brain

You told me of setting your hand
into the print of a long-dead Indian
and for a moment, I knew that hand,

that print, that rock,
that sun producing powerful dreams
A word can do this

or, as tonight, the mirror of the fire
of my mind, burning as if it could go on
burning itself, burning down

feeding on everything
till there is nothing in life
that has not fed that fire

1972

For a Sister

> *Natalya Gorbanevskaya, two years*
> *incarcerated in a Soviet penal mental asylum*
> *for her political activism; and others.*

I trust none of them. Only my existence
thrown out in the world like a towchain
battered and twisted in many chance connections,
being pulled this way, pulling in that.

I have to steal the sense of dust on your floor,
milk souring in your pantry
after they came and took you.
I'm forced to guess at the look you threw backward.

A few paragraphs in the papers,
allowing for printers' errors, wilful omissions,
the trained violence of doctors.
I don't trust them, but I'm learning how to use them.

Little by little out of the blurred conjectures
your face clears, a sunken marble
slowly cranked up from underwater.
I feel the ropes straining under their load of despair.

They searched you for contraband, they made their notations.
A look of intelligence could get you twenty years.
Better to trace nonexistent circles with your finger,
try to imitate the smile of the permanently dulled.

My images. This metaphor for what happens.
A geranium in flames on a green cloth
becomes yours. You, coming home after years
to light the stove, get out the typewriter and begin again. Your story.

1972

From a Survivor

The pact that we made was the ordinary pact
of men & women in those days

I don't know who we thought we were
that our personalities
could resist the failures of the race

Lucky or unlucky, we didn't know
the race had failures of that order
and that we were going to share them

Like everybody else, we thought of ourselves as special

Your body is as vivid to me
as it ever was: even more

since my feeling for it is clearer:
I know what it could and could not do

it is no longer
the body of a god
or anything with power over my life

Next year it would have been 20 years
and you are wastefully dead
who might have made the leap
we talked, too late, of making

which I live now
not as a leap
but a succession of brief, amazing movements

each one making possible the next

1972

August

Two horses in yellow light
eating windfall apples under a tree

as summer tears apart   milkweeds stagger
and grasses grow more ragged

They say there are ions in the sun
neutralizing magnetic fields on earth

Some way to explain
what this week has been, and the one before it!

If I am flesh sunning on rock
if I am brain burning in fluorescent light

if I am dream like a wire with fire
throbbing along it

if I am death to man
I have to know it

His mind is too simple, I cannot go on
sharing his nightmares

My own are becoming clearer, they open
into prehistory

which looks like a village lit with blood
where all the fathers are crying: *My son is mine!*

1972

Meditations for a Savage Child

The prose passages are from J.-M. Itard's account of The Wild Boy of Aveyron, *as translated by G. and M. Humphrey.*

There was a profound indifference to the objects of our pleasures and of our fictitious needs; there was still . . . so intense a passion for the freedom of the fields . . . that he would certainly have escaped into the forest had not the most rigid precautions been taken . . .

In their own way, by their own lights
they tried to care for you
tried to teach you to care
for objects of their caring:
                    glossed oak planks, glass
                    whirled in a fire
                    to impossible thinness

to teach you names
for things
you did not need

                muslin shirred against the sun
                linen on a sack of feathers
                locks, keys
                boxes with coins inside

they tried to make you feel
the importance of

                a piece of cowhide
                sewn around a bundle
                of leaves impressed with signs

to teach you language:
the thread their lives
were strung on

II

*When considered from a more general and philosophic point of
view, these scars bear witness . . . against the feebleness and in-
sufficiency of man when left entirely to himself, and in favor of the
resources of nature which . . . work openly to repair and conserve
that which she tends secretly to impair and destroy.*

I keep thinking about the lesson of the human ear
which stands for music, which stands for balance—
or the cat's ear which I can study better
the whorls and ridges exposed
It seems a hint dropped about the inside of the skull
which I cannot see
lobe, zone, that part of the brain
which is pure survival

The most primitive part
I go back into at night
pushing the leathern curtain
with naked fingers
then
with naked body

There where every wound is registered
as scar tissue

A cave of scars!
ancient, archaic wallpaper
built up, layer on layer
from the earliest, dream-white
to yesterday's, a red-black scrawl
a red mouth slowly closing

Go back so far there is another language
go back far enough the language
is no longer personal

these scars bear witness
but whether to repair
or to destruction
I no longer know

III

It is true that there is visible on the throat a very extended scar which might throw some doubt upon the soundness of the underlying parts if one were not reassured by the appearance of the scar . . .

When I try to speak
my throat is cut
and, it seems, by his hand

The sounds I make are prehuman, radical
the telephone is always
ripped-out

and he sleeps on
Yet always the tissue
grows over, white as silk

hardly a blemish
maybe a hieroglyph for scream

Child, no wonder you never wholly
trusted your keepers

IV

A hand with the will rather than the habit of crime had wished
to make an attempt on the life of this child . . . left for dead in
the woods, he will have owed the prompt recovery of his wound to
the help of nature alone.

In the 18th century infanticide
reaches epidemic proportions:
old prints attest to it: starving mothers
smothering babies in sleep
abandoning newborns in sleet
on the poorhouse steps
gin-blurred, setting fire to the room

I keep thinking of the flights we used to take
on the grapevine across the gully
littered with beer-bottles where dragonflies flashed
we were 10, 11 years old
wild little girls with boyish bodies
flying over the moist
shadow-mottled earth
till they warned us to stay away from there

Later they pointed out
the venetian blinds
of the abortionist's house
we shivered

Men can do things to you
was all they said

V

And finally, my Lord, looking at this long experiment . . . whether
it be considered as the methodical education of a savage or as no
more than the physical and moral treatment of one of those creatures
ill-favored by nature, rejected by society and abandoned by medi-

cine, the care that has been taken and ought still to be taken of him, the changes that have taken place, and those that can be hoped for, the voice of humanity, the interest inspired by such a desertion and a destiny so strange—all these things recommend this extraordinary young man to the attention of scientists, to the solicitude of administrators, and to the protection of the government.

1. The doctor in "Uncle Vanya":
   They will call us fools,
   blind, ignorant, they will
   despise us

   devourers of the forest
   leaving teeth of metal in every tree
   so the tree can neither grow
   nor be cut for lumber

   Does the primeval forest
   weep
   for its devourers

   does nature mourn
   our existence

   is the child with arms
   burnt to the flesh of its sides
   weeping eyelessly for man

2. At the end of the distinguished doctor's
   lecture
   a young woman raises her hand:

   You have the power
   in your hands, you control our lives—
   why do you want our pity too?

   Why are men afraid
   why do you pity yourselves
   why do the administrators

lack solicitude, the government
refuse protection,

why should the wild child
weep for the scientists

why

1972

Poems

1973–1974

Essential Resources

I don't know
how late it is. I'm writing
with a chewed blunted lead
under a bridge while snow blankets the city
or with a greasy ballpoint
the nurse left
in a ward of amnesiacs who can be trusted
not to take notes

You talk of a film we could make
with women's faces naked
of make-up, the mist of sweat
on a forehead, lips dry
the little bloodspot from a coldsore

I know the inmates are encouraged
to express themselves
I'm wondering how

I long to create something
that can't be used to keep us passive:
I want to write
a script about plumbing, how every pipe
is joined
to every other

the wash of pure water and sewage
side by side

or about the electrical system
a study of the sources of energy
till in the final shot
the whole screen goes dark
and the keepers of order are screaming

I forget
what year it is. I am thinking
of films we have made but cannot show
yet, films of the mind unfolding
and our faces, still young
sweated with desire and
premature clarity

1973

Blood-Sister

—for Cynthia

Shoring up the ocean. A railroad track
ran close to the coast for miles
through the potato-fields, bringing us
to summer. Weeds blur the ties,
sludge clots the beaches.

During the war, the shells we found—
salmon-and-silver coins
sand dollars dripping sand
like dust. We were dressed
in navy dotted-swiss dresses in the train
not to show the soot. Like dolls
we sat with our dolls in the station.

When did we begin to dress ourselves?

Now I'm wearing jeans spider-webbed
with creases, a black sweater bought years ago
worn almost daily since
the ocean has undergone a tracheotomy
and lost its resonance
you wear a jersey the color of

Navaho turquoise and sand
you are holding a naked baby girl
she laughs into your eyes
we sit at your table drinking coffee
light flashes off unwashed sheetglass
you are more beautiful than you have ever been

we talk of destruction and creation
ice fits itself around each twig of the lilac
like a fist of law and order
your imagination burns like a bulb in the frozen soil
the fierce shoots knock
at the roof of waiting

when summer comes the ocean may be closed for good
we will turn
to the desert
where survival
takes naked and fiery forms

1973

The Wave

—for J.B.

To give you back this wave
I would have to give back
the black
spaces

fretted with film of spray,
darker and deeper than the mind
they are emblems of

Not only the creator fury
of the whitest churn

the caldron of all life
but the blankness underlying

Thinking of the sea I think of light
lacing, lancing the water
the blue knife of a radiant consciousness
bent by the waves of vision as it pierces
to the deepest grotto

And I think of those lives we tried to live
in our globed helmets, self-enclosed
bodies self-illumined gliding
safe from the turbulence

and how, miraculously, we failed

1973

The Fourth Month of the Landscape Architect

It is asleep in my body.
For now, I am myself,
like anyone, like a man
whose body contains simply: itself.
I draw a too-big sweater
over my breasts, walk into the drafting-room
and stand there, balancing.
The sun sprays acid points of light
on the tools of my trade, the metal,
the edged instruments. My work has always been
with edges. For a while I listen:
will there be a knock, is the neighbor
so near me stirring behind his walls?
The neighbor is quiet. I am not

a body, I am no body, I am I,
a pair of hands ending in fingers
that think like a brain.
I draw a sheet of paper toward me
on the slanted drafting-table.
I start to imagine
plans for a house, a park
stretching in every direction to the horizon
which is no horizon
which is merely a circle of volcanoes.
I touch stylus, T-square, pens
of immeasurable fineness,
the hard-edge. I am I,
this India ink my rain
which can irrigate gardens, terraces
dissolve or project horizons
flowing like lava from the volcano of the inkpot
at the stirring of my mind.
A city waits at the back of my skull
eating its heart out to be born:
how design the first
city of the moon? how shall I see it
for all of us who are done
with enclosed spaces, purdah, the salon, the sweatshop loft,
the ingenuity of the cloister?
My mind flies at the moon
beating, a pale-green kite.
Something else is beating.
In my body.
Spaces fold in. I'm caught
in the enclosure of the crib my body
where every thought I think
simply loosens to life another life.

1973

The Alleged Murderess
Walking in Her Cell

Nine months we conspired:
first in panic, then in a quieter dread,
finally an unfamiliar kind of peace.
In the new year voices began,
they said I'd helped beat a man to death,
even my lover said so.
You were no bigger than a cyst
then, a bead of life
lit from within.
I took that life in my hands
with mine; a key turned
and the voices shrank away.
Then began that whispered conversation
telling each other we were alive,
twins in the prison womb,
exchanging vows against the future.
Justice, they say, and clemency
installed our nursery in the house
of detention. I don't know what
it means, that we have each other.
Do they mean to—can they use you
against me? I walk up and down
more at peace than in any prison night
here or outside—
your warmth washing into my ribcage
your frail silken skull asleep against my throat
your anxious pleading stilled—
unable to remember
whether or not I ever killed
whether I ever lived
without this—the blue pulse of your life
with its blind stroke: *Not-Guilty*

fledging my twenty-one-year life
of unmeaning, my worthless life
they framed in their contempt.

1973

Re-forming the Crystal

I am trying to imagine
how it feels to you
to want a woman

trying to hallucinate
desire
centered in a cock
focused like a burning-glass

desire without discrimination:
to want a woman like a fix

Desire: yes: the sudden knowledge, like coming out of 'flu, that the
body is sexual. Walking in the streets with that knowledge. That
evening in the plane from Pittsburgh, fantasizing going to meet
you. Walking through the airport blazing with energy and joy. But
knowing all along that you were not the source of that energy and
joy; you were a man, a stranger, a name, a voice on the telephone,
a friend; this desire was mine, this energy my energy; it could be
used a hundred ways, and going to meet you could be one of them.

Tonight is a different kind of night.
I sit in the car, racing the engine,
calculating the thinness of the ice.
In my head I am already threading the beltways
that rim this city,
all the old roads that used to wander the country
having been lost.

Tonight I understand
my photo on the license is not me,
my
name on the marriage-contract was not mine.
If I remind you of my father's favorite daughter,
look again. The woman
I needed to call my mother
was silenced before I was born.

Tonight if the battery charges I want to take the car out on sheet-
ice; I want to understand my fear both of the machine and of the
accidents of nature. My desire for you is not trivial; I can compare
it with the greatest of those accidents. But the energy it draws on
might lead to racing a cold engine, cracking the frozen spiderweb,
parachuting into the field of a poem wired with danger, or to a trip
through gorges and canyons, into the cratered night of female mem-
ory, where delicately and with intense care the chieftainess in-
scribes upon the ribs of the volcano the name of the one she has
chosen.

1973

White Night

Light at a window. Someone up
at this snail-still hour.
We who work this way have often worked
in solitude. I've had to guess at her
sewing her skin together as I sew mine
though
with a different
stitch.

Dawn after dawn, this neighbor
burns like a candle
dragging her bedspread through the dark house

to her dark bed
her head
full of runes, syllables, refrains,
this accurate dreamer

sleepwalks the kitchen
like a white moth,
an elephant, a guilt.
Somebody tried to put her
to rest under an afghan
knitted with wools the color of grass and blood

but she has risen. Her lamplight
licks at the icy panes
and melts into the dawn.
They will never prevent her
who sleep the stone sleep of the past,
the sleep of the drugged.
One crystal second, I flash

an eye across the cold
unwrapping of light between us
into her darkness-lancing eye
—that's all. Dawn is the test, the agony
but we were meant to see it:
After this, we may sleep, my sister,
while the flames rise higher and higher, we can sleep.

1974

Amnesia

I almost trust myself to know
when we're getting to that scene—
call it the snow-scene in *Citizen Kane:*

the mother handing over her son
the earliest American dream
shot in a black-and-white

where every flake of snow
is incandescent
with its own burden, adding-

up, always adding-up to the
cold blur of the past
But first there is the picture of the past

simple and pitiless as the deed
truly was
the putting-away of a childish thing

Becoming a man means leaving
someone, or something—
still, why

must the snow-scene blot itself out
the flakes come down so fast
so heavy, so unrevealing

over the something that gets left behind?

1974

Family Romance

(*the brothers speak*)

Our mother went away and our father was the king
always absent at the wars

We had to make it together or not at all
in the black forest

cutting paths, stumbling on the witch's house
long empty

gathering wood and mushrooms, gathering everything
we needed in a wordless collusion

Sometimes we pretended the witch had been our mother
and would come back

we loved each other with a passion understood
like the great roots of the wood

In another country we might have fought each other
and died of fraternal wounds

conspiring each alone for the father's blessing,
the birthright, the mother

Since we had no father to bless us, we were free
and our birthright was each other

our life was harsh and simple; we slept deeply
and we thought our mother came and watched us sleeping

1974

The Fact of a Doorframe

means there is something to hold
onto with both hands
while slowly thrusting my forehead against the wood
and taking it away
one of the oldest motions of suffering
as Makeba sings
a courage-song for warriors

music is suffering made powerful

I think of the story
of the goose-girl who passed through the high gate
where the head of her favorite mare
was nailed to the arch
and in a human voice
If she could see thee now, thy mother's heart would break
said the head
of Falada

Now, again, poetry,
violent, arcane, common,
hewn of the commonest living substance
into archway, portal, frame
I grasp for you, your bloodstained splinters, your
ancient and stubborn poise
—as the earth trembles—
burning out from the grain

1974

For L.G.: Unseen for Twenty Years

A blue-grained line circles a fragment of the mind
drawn in ancient crayon:
out of the blue, your tightstrung smile—

often in the first snow
that even here smells only of itself
even on this Broadway limped by cripples
and the self-despising
Still, in that smell, another snow,
another world: we're walking
grey boulevards traced with white

in Paris, the early 'fifties
of invincible ignorance:

or, a cold spring:
I clasp your hips on the bike
shearing the empty plain in March
teeth gritted in the wind
searching for Chartres:
we doze
in the boat-train

we who were friends and thought
women and men should be lovers

Your face: taut as a mask of wires, a fencer's mask
half-turned away, the one night, walking
the City of Love, so cold
we warmed our nerves with wine
at every all-night café
to keep on walking, talking
Your words have drifted back for twenty years:

I have to tell you—maybe I'm not a man—
I can't do it with women—but I'd like
to hold you, to know what it's like
to sleep and wake together—

the one night in all our weeks of talk
you talked of fear
                    I wonder

what words of mine drift back to you?
Something like:
                    But you're a man, I know it—
the swiftness of your mind is masculine—?

—some set-piece I'd learned to embroider
in my woman's education
while the needle scarred my hand?

Of course, you're a man. I like you. What else could you be?
what else, what else,
what bloody else . . .

Given the cruelty of our times and customs,
maybe you hate these memories,
the ignorance, the innocence we shared:
maybe you cruise the SoHo cocktail parties
the Vancouver bar-scene
stalking yourself as I can see you still:
young, tense, amorphous, longing—

maybe you live out your double life
in the Berkeley hills, with a wife
who stuns her mind into indifference
with Scotch and saunas
while you arrange your own humiliations
downtown

(and, yes, I've played my scenes
of favorite daughter, child-bride, token woman, muse
listening now and then
as a drunken poet muttered into my hair:
I can't make it with women I admire—)

maybe you've found or fought
through to a kind of faithfulness
in the strange coexistence
of two of any gender

But we were talking in 1952
of the fear of being cripples in a world
of perfect women and men:
we were the givens and the stake
and we did badly

and, dear heart, I know, had a lover gestured
you'd have left me
for a man, as I left you,
as we left each other, seeking the love of men.

1974

From an Old House in America

1.

Deliberately, long ago
the carcasses

of old bugs crumbled
into the rut of the window

and we started sleeping here
Fresh June bugs batter this June's

screens, June-lightning batters
the spiderweb

I sweep the wood-dust
from the wood-box

the snout of the vacuum cleaner
sucks the past away

2.

Other lives were lived here:
mostly un-articulate

yet someone left her creamy signature
in the trail of rusticated

narcissus straggling up
through meadowgrass and vetch

Families breathed close
boxed-in from the cold

hard times, short growing season
the old rainwater cistern

hulks in the cellar

3.

Like turning through the contents of a drawer:
these rusted screws, this empty vial

useless, this box of watercolor paints
dried to insolubility—

but this—
this pack of cards with no card missing

still playable
and three good fuses

and this toy: a little truck
scarred red, yet all its wheels still turn

The humble tenacity of things
waiting for people, waiting for months, for years

4.

Often rebuked, yet always back returning
I place my hand on the hand

of the dead, invisible palm-print
on the doorframe

spiked with daylilies, green leaves
catching in the screen door

or I read the backs of old postcards
curling from thumbtacks, winter and summer

fading through cobweb-tinted panes—
white church in Norway

Dutch hyacinths bleeding azure
red beach on Corsica

set-pieces of the world
stuck to this house of plank

I flash on wife and husband
embattled, in the years

that dried, dim ink was wet
those signatures

5.

If they call me man-hater, you
would have known it for a lie

but the *you* I want to speak to
has become your death

If I dream of you these days
I know my dreams are mine and not of you

yet something hangs between us
older and stranger than ourselves

like a translucent curtain, a sheet of water
a dusty window

the irreducible, incomplete connection
between the dead and living

or between man and woman in this
savagely fathered and unmothered world

6.

The other side of a translucent
curtain, a sheet of water

a dusty window, Non-being
utters its flat tones

the speech of an actor learning his lines
phonetically

the final autistic statement
of the self-destroyer

All my energy reaches out tonight
to comprehend a miracle beyond

raising the dead: the undead to watch
back on the road of birth

7.

I am an American woman:
I turn that over

like a leaf pressed in a book
I stop and look up from

into the coals of the stove
or the black square of the window

Foot-slogging through the Bering Strait
jumping from the *Arbella* to my death

chained to the corpse beside me
I feel my pains begin

I am washed up on this continent
shipped here to be fruitful

my body a hollow ship
bearing sons to the wilderness

sons who ride away
on horseback, daughters

whose juices drain like mine
into the *arroyo* of stillbirths, massacres

Hanged as witches, sold as breeding-wenches
my sisters leave me

I am not the wheatfield
nor the virgin forest

I never chose this place
yet I am of it now

In my decent collar, in the daguerrotype
I pierce its legend with my look

my hands wring the necks of prairie chickens
I am used to blood

When the men hit the hobo track
I stay on with the children

my power is brief and local
but I know my power

I have lived in isolation
from other women, so much

in the mining camps, the first cities
the Great Plains winters

Most of the time, in my sex, I was alone

8.

Tonight in this northeast kingdom
striated iris stand in a jar with daisies

the porcupine gnaws in the shed
fireflies beat and simmer

caterpillars begin again
their long, innocent climb

the length of leaves of burdock
or webbing of a garden chair

plain and ordinary things
speak softly

the light square on old wallpaper
where a poster has fallen down

Robert Indiana's LOVE
leftover of a decade

9.

I do not want to simplify
Or: I would simplify

by naming the complexity
It was made over-simple all along

the separation of powers
the allotment of sufferings

her spine cracking in labor
his plow driving across the Indian graves

her hand unconscious on the cradle, her mind
with the wild geese

his mother-hatred driving him
into exile from the earth

the refugee couple with their cardboard luggage
standing on the ramshackle landing-stage

he with fingers frozen around his Law
she with her down quilt sewn through iron nights

—the weight of the old world, plucked
drags after them, a random feather-bed

10.

Her children dead of diphtheria, she
set herself on fire with kerosene

(O Lord I was unworthy
Thou didst find me out)

she left the kitchen scrubbed
down to the marrow of its boards

"The penalty for barrenness
is emptiness

my punishment is my crime
what I have failed to do, is me . . ."

—Another month without a show
and this the seventh year

O Father let this thing pass out of me
I swear to You

I will live for the others, asking nothing
I will ask nothing, ever, for myself

11.

Out back of this old house
datura tangles with a gentler weed

its spiked pods smelling
of bad dreams and death

I reach through the dark, groping
past spines of nightmare

to brush the leaves of sensuality
A dream of tenderness

wrestles with all I know of history
I cannot now lie down

with a man who fears my power
or reaches for me as for death

or with a lover who imagines
we are not in danger

12.

If it was lust that had defined us—
their lust and fear of our deep places

we have done our time
as faceless torsos licked by fire

we are in the open, on our way—
our counterparts

the pinyon jay, the small
gilt-winged insect

the Cessna throbbing level
the raven floating in the gorge

the rose and violet vulva of the earth
filling with darkness

yet deep within a single sparkle
of red, a human fire

and near and yet above the western planet
calmly biding her time

13.

They were the distractions, lust and fear
but are

themselves a key
Everything that can be used, will be:

the fathers in their ceremonies
the genital contests

the cleansing of blood from pubic hair
the placenta buried and guarded

their terror of blinding
by the look of her who bore them

If you do not believe
that fear and hatred

read the lesson again
in the old dialect

14.

But can't you see me as a human being
he said

What is a human being
she said

I try to understand
he said

what will you undertake
she said

will you punish me for history
he said

what will you undertake
she said

do you believe in collective guilt
he said

let me look in your eyes
she said

15.

Who is here. The Erinyes.
One to sit in judgment.

One to speak tenderness.
One to inscribe the verdict on the canyon wall.

If you have not confessed
the damage

if you have not recognized
the Mother of reparations

if you have not come to terms
with the women in the mirror

if you have not come to terms
with the inscription

the terms of the ordeal
the discipline   the verdict

if still you are on your way
still She awaits your coming

16.

"Such women are dangerous
to the order of things"

and yes, we will be dangerous
to ourselves

groping through spines of nightmare
(*datura* tangling with a simpler herb)

because the line dividing
lucidity from darkness

is yet to be marked out

Isolation, the dream
of the frontier woman

leveling her rifle along
the homestead fence

still snares our pride
—a suicidal leaf

laid under the burning-glass
in the sun's eye

Any woman's death diminishes me

1974

Notes

THE DIAMOND CUTTERS

The Tourist and the Town. The pronouns in the third part of the poem were originally masculine. But the tourist was a woman, myself, and I never saw her as anything else. In 1953, when the poem was written, some notion of "universality" prevailed which made the feminine pronoun suspect, "personal." In this poem, and in "Afterward" in *A Change of World,* I have altered the pronouns not simply as a matter of fact but because they alter, for me, the dimensions of the poem.

Villa Adriana. The summer palace built by the Emperor Hadrian for his favorite boy, Antinoüs. In "Antinoüs: The Diaries" I let the young man speak for me.

The Snow Queen. Hans Christian Andersen's tale was the point of departure for the poem.

SNAPSHOTS OF A DAUGHTER-IN-LAW

Euryclea's Tale. Euryclea was the old nurse of Odysseus and the first person to recognize him when he returned home from his wanderings.

Snapshots of a Daughter-in-Law. The quoted lines in Part 7 were written by Mary Wollstonecraft (*Thoughts on the Education of Daughters,* London, 1787.)

NECESSITIES OF LIFE

In the Woods. The first line is borrowed and translated from the Dutch poet J. C. Bloem.

I Am in Danger—Sir—. See the *Letters of Emily Dickinson,*
T. H. Johnson, ed., Vol. II, p. 409.

LEAFLETS

Orion. One or two phrases suggested by Gottfried Benn's essay,
"Artists and Old Age" in *Primal Vision,* edited by E. B. Ash-
ton.

Charleston in the Eighteen-Sixties. See Ben Ames Williams' se-
lections from Mary Chesnut's diaries in *A Diary from Dixie.*

The Observer. Suggested by a brief newspaper account of the
fieldwork of Diane Fossey.

For A Russian Poet. Part 3 is based on an account by Natalya
Gorbanevskaya of a protest action against the Soviet invasion
of Czechoslovakia.

Leaflets. "The love of a fellow-creature in all its fullness con-
sists simply in the ability to say to him, 'What are you going
through?' "—Simone Weil.

Ghazals: Homage to Ghalib. This poem began to be written
after I read Aijaz Ahmad's literal English versions of the Urdu
poetry of Mirza Ghalib (1797–1869). While the structure and
metrics of the classic *ghazal* form as used by Ghalib are much
stricter than mine, I adhered to his use of a minimum five
couplets to a *ghazal,* each couplet being autonomous and inde-
pendent of the others. The continuity and unity flow from the
associations and images playing back and forth among the
couplets in any single *ghazal.* I have left the *ghazals* dated as
I wrote them, during a month in the summer of 1968.

NEW POEMS

From an Old House in America. Part 4: the first line is bor-
rowed from a poem, "Stanzas," by Emily Brontë.

Part 7: Many African women went into labor and gave birth

on the slave-ships of the Middle Passage, chained for the duration of the voyage to the dying or the dead.

Part 11: *Datura* is a poisonous hallucinogenic weed. It has a spiky green pod and a white flower, and is also known as jimson-weed, or deadly nightshade.

Index